HIGH
Yields
for
HIGH
Heels

A LADY'S GUIDE
TO INVESTING

Tellwell Talent
www.tellwell.ca

ISBN
978-1-77370-426-5 (Hardcover)
978-1-77370-425-8 (Paperback)
978-1-77370-427-2 (eBook)

Contents

Preface

I am a grumpy old man, 78 years of age. I wasn't always so, however having seen the indignities suffered by a number of my lady friends I can't help but be. A number of these ladies have made a small fortune in the stock market. Regrettably they started with a large fortune. Their financial advisors or stockbrokers, forever seeking higher returns and profits (for themselves), have had the temerity to purchase for the portfolios of these ladies, mining company shares, real estate limited partnerships and junior oil companies securities. These are wonderful speculations for the 30 something market cowboys but completely out of line for the mature woman. If you are a senior citizen you don't care if the market is hitting new highs or lows, you want to know that the interest and dividend cheques that are supporting your lifestyle are continuing to fall – into your mailbox. In deep despair, a number of ladies of indeterminate age asked me to review their portfolios and explain what it all means to them. What I had to tell one of them was that her $5 million in capital that could have easily thrown off $300,000 in interest annually had been reduced to a portfolio of $3 million which is providing $180,000 a year.

Let me give you a case example. When Mrs. B. was 68 in her portfolio there were holdings like Allstate, Best Buy, First Chicago Energy, Oilexco and Sunstone Opportunities (an illiquid, limited partnership type of investment). As you can see this portfolio of low or no dividend stocks would likely double or triple in the next twenty years. Mrs. B would be delirious with joy after having lived on peanut butter and Kraft Dinners all that time to experience those massive capital gains. There is one very tenuous assumption in all this. No, the portfolio will be worth substantially more, but it is unlikely Mrs. B. will be around to enjoy it. In fact if she were to die at the time of this writing, her estate would have difficulty settling as there is no market for the Sunstone investment. Her estate would be left unexecuted until the Sunstone could be liquidated or more likely executed.

How can this happen? The broker gets a new account as a result of the existing broker leaving the business for whatever reason. The new guy is really new. He's never seen a depression (nor have his parents) or a serious recession. He's just bought his first Porsche and is in the bar most nights after work hearing of the exploits of the great recent investment gurus (this was before they were criminally and civilly charged). He arrived at his office the next morning and called the lady pensioner. The conversation went something like this:

> "Mrs. B. it's Thomas Turnover calling. I've taken over for old Mr. Steadyhand who ran your portfolio. Mr. Steadyhand was a fine gentleman, but a little behind the times. I see his most recent purchase for you was some Bell Canada bonds that will only yield 6% to maturity, and that at a time when stocks are doubling and tripling every year. Look at those commodity funds and the smart guys like Madoff, Bloom or Manor who are bringing in 10 or 13% capital gains every year. Let me mention that these are profits that are subject to lower taxation, unlike your fully taxable bond interest. Also, I can unequivocally say that stocks outperform bonds."

At this point Turnover uttered the four most dangerous words in the investment industry.

"*This time it's different.* Copper is $5.00 a pound because of China and India. They can't just stop buying. Their economies would collapse."

Thomas Turnover had not conceived of the scenario where the Chinese and Indian economies would collapse first and then they would stop buying $5.00 a pound copper. But Thomas Turnover was a desperate man. He needed only one more high net worth client to be able to justify the down payment for that new 45 foot Hinckley sail boat which would be the biggest sail boat at his yacht club. His old Bavaria 41 foot sloop had been the biggest and then the advisor from Raymond James had bought a 43 foot Hunter which left Turnover feeling degraded.

Turnover prevailed and Mrs. B. opened an investment account which did 47 trades in one year and the new yacht was delivered in April, just in time for the sailing season. I was asked as a retired investment executive (I had been a top ranked analyst, partner in a stellar institutional stock brokerage and a director of another innovative firm) by Mrs. B. to explain to her why her portfolio was worth 60% of what it had been.

The explanation was painful, so much so, that Mrs. B. organized a number of diners at fine restaurants so that I could explain to her friends who were also mature women how they might save their nest eggs from being fried. This book was derived from those chats. The reason for those chats was because there was another villain in this set piece, the husband/consort.

Few male mates make the effort to inform their partners about investment matters. They fear that it would be distasteful, difficult and possibly lead to the shortening of their lives. So when good old

Ralph goes off to the great golf course in the sky his mate is left with a pot of money and no idea of what to do with it.

I can assure any of the gentlemen reading this book that teaching your mate about investing is not the chore you imagine it to be and in fact it is your responsibility seeing as you were born into the sex that will die first. As you know what you want to instill is the concept that she wants a return on her assets and how to achieve that. It may in fact prolong your life as my mate has learned that the investing of money is so essential that she is attempting to make me immortal.

Introduction

There are two types of stock market participants, the willing and the unwilling. The willing are actually masquerading. These impostors buy shares because they know their prices will increase and they will make massive amounts of money because they are the only ones who know of this forthcoming event. Sadly the overseers of the markets insist that all the relevant knowledge regarding a company and its shares be released to the public and the miraculous event expected is already reflected in the pricing of the shares. These impostors are labeled by the real investing community with the technical term, "speculators". For them, like the gambling addict, there is no future except penury.

The second type of investor and the most prevalent is the unwilling. He or she is forced into the position of having to place current excessive productivity in some vehicle for the day when they will produce less than they consume. These people will be in a constant state of concern over whether or not their choices for a parking place for these excess funds represents a safe and remunerative home for their assets. The options open to these people are to own a piece of a business (a shareholding) or to loan money to someone's business for interest (a bond holding). These people do not see their investments as a sure road to early retirement. They hope that their investments will be sufficient to support them in the style they have become accustomed to. That does not seem a lot to ask and yet there are many who won't achieve that goal.

The reason that some do not achieve what is a well-defined and simple goal is that they are not professionals in the arcane art of investing. They have no interest or skill in determining the ratio of share price to book value of a share or the interest coverage of a bond. All they want is some professional to find secure investments with a reasonable return. But therein lays the problem. What is that investment professional to do after he has found that long term home for the client's money? What is such a service worth? How should it be paid for, with a fee or commissions? Should the earnings of the professional be based on the performance of the portfolio or on the volume of trading it can generate?

There is an answer and like all good answers it is a simple one. However before you can have the answer, like a detective novel you'll have to meet all the characters, sift through evidence and read through to the end to find the truth. Let's start at the beginning.

In The Beginning

It was a warm spring evening on a small farm outside of Athens around 420 BC. Sophia and Dmitri had just sat down for dinner when she raised a question.

> "Dmitri, when I was cleaning up today I found a leather pouch under the mattress and there were over a thousand drachmas[1] in it. What is that all about?"

> "Well my dear, unlike you, I am growing older and I believe there will come a time when we can no longer work the farm. Over the past few years our farm has produced more than we consumed and I have kept that as saving for the day we retire."

> "I like the sounds of that Dmitri, but why not put the money to work."

> "I can't see the money tending the flocks or harvesting crops. What possibly can you mean?"

---

1   The Greek Drachma was the reserve currency of the world for about 800 years and was accepted worldwide similarly to the US dollar today, and the British pound 100 years ago.

"We can make the money work for us by buying more animals or land. What we make from that we could then use to buy even more productive things."

"Great idea. I'll go to agora[2] tomorrow and see what's available." And so investing was born.

Over the years Dmitri and Sophia continued to re-invest the profits from their ever increasing farming enterprise and were pricing out retirement villas near Cape Sounion and in the Aegean Islands as they had discovered, as Einstein called it, the eighth wonder of the world, compound interest.[3] This was the concept that you could earn money on the money you previously earned in a never ending cycle of increased profitability. However, there was danger lurking on the road to the heavens at Olympus.

While Dmitri was milking one of their goats a man came strolling up to him. The man was dressed in a really snappy looking pinstriped toga with a silk Hermes sash and wearing a pair of patent leather Gucci sandals. He appeared to be a man of substance and his name was Kleptis. The goat he was leading on a silk tether could only be described as gorgeous.

"Allow me to introduce myself, I am Kleptis of Crete, and you are?"

"Just plain Dmitri."

"Dmitri, this is indeed your lucky day. Look at this goat, Sylvia. What do you think of her?"

"By Zeus, she is the most beautiful goat I have ever seen."

---

2   The Agora was the ancient Athenian market.

3   "compound interest is eighth wonder of the world. He who understands it, earns it, he who doesn't, pays it." Einstein

"Well, Dmitri, I am a little short of cash and would be willing to part with this gorgeous beast for a paltry ten drachmas."

"I will admit she is a beauty but to make that kind of investment I would have to ask Sophia, my wife."

Dmitri dragged Sophia away from churning butter and showed her the goat.

"Is she not the most beautiful goat you have ever seen? Kleptis, here, only wants ten drachmas for her."

"How many kids has she produced?" Sophia asked.

"None, she is barren," was Kleptis reply.

"And how many liters of milk can we expect per day from her?"

"She's dry," he responded.

"Wait just a minute why would you expect us to pay ten drachmas for a dry, barren goat?"

"Madam, there is a shortage of beautiful goats developing here in Greece, in fact in the known world. I have a report from our research department that says this phenomenon could lead to the doubling of the price of beautiful goats within a year. Our target price for beautiful goats is 20 drachmas. The conclusion is even supported by the Delphic Oracle which confirms that the price of beautiful goats is going up. If you pay me ten drachmas for the goat you can take her down the road tomorrow and sell her for much more."

"Let me see that research report," Sophia snorted. Kleptis handed over the scroll which Sophia quickly scanned.

"Ah here it is, the Delphic Oracle. The Oracle says the market for beautiful goats will fluctuate."

"Of course," Kleptis replied," that means that it will go up".

"And down as well," Sophia retorted. "No thank you, Mr. Kleptis. This sounds like, as the Romans call it, a speculari."

As Kleptis sauntered off leading the beautiful Sylvia, Dmitri asked, "Sophia I don't know much Latin. What does 'speculari' mean in plain Greek?"

"It means to 'spy out' or in other words know what is not known, like how much higher the price of beautiful goats will go before collapsing as most speculations must. What Kleptis was offering is not as you originally thought an investment."

This was how I got the point across to the ladies about the difference between investing and speculating. With an investment you want a constant return for the use of your money be it in milk or olives. You might even place your money with someone else to use and charge him rent for your money or as we call it today, interest, but the defining character of an investment is that it provides the investor a reliable and definable return on a continuing basis.

A speculation on the other hand is something that is bought with the hope that it can be sold for a higher price. There is nothing that foretells that higher price, there is only expectation or hope. Another distinction which should be made is gambling versus speculation. Speculation is a decision based on the assessment of known facts to determine the outcome of a future event. Gambling is the participation in a game of chance where the outcome cannot be foretold. If someone tossing coins throws four heads in a row there is nothing to indicate that the next outcome will be either heads or tails. If you wager money on the next outcome you are gambling. If you read the papers and conclude that there will be war in the Middle East you can purchase oil company shares assuming that the oil price will rise as a result of the war. You would be speculating on how you expect current events to influence the future.

At this point I should probably remark on Greek women's names. They are truly beautiful such as Zoe which means life, Alethia meaning truth, Agape means love and Sophia means wisdom. As for men's names, Kleptis means thief.

The Birth Of A Company

It was as usual, a rainy afternoon in May of 1670's London, when Prince Rupert's secretary announced to the Prince, who was playing whist at the time, that he had an appointment to see two gentlemen from the City[4].

"Ah yes, I completely forgot. I'll see them as soon as I finish this hand."

Having dismissed his opponents his supplicants were ushered in.

"What might I do for you?" the Prince asked.

"Sire, you are truly close to the Monarch's ear and what we are seeking is the exclusive right to trade into the area of Hudson's Bay in Canada. A privilege only the Monarch can bestow."

"What would you do with such a privilege?"

"We would raise a sum of money with which we would buy goods to trade with the natives of that area for their

---

4 The "City" referred to an area in London where there were a number locations where people transacted financial business.

very valuable furs. We all would share in the venture to the extent that we provided funding. We are to call this undertaking 'A Company of Adventurers Trading into Hudson's Bay'."

"If I should obtain this benefit for you what will accrue to me?" the Prince asked.

"Sire, we will name the area after you and call it "Rupert's Land'."

"Gentlemen, you may think that as a result of my family's inbreeding that I am stupid. That is not true. I may be crazy but not stupid. Why would I give you such a privilege and take nothing for myself when the privilege could make you immensely wealthy? No, gentlemen, here is my proposal. I will obtain that right for you but I expect to have a free 25 percent interest or share or we can call it a shareholding, whatever. I suspect that my 25 percent will be the largest shareholding therefore I will want to have a representative of mine directing the affairs of the entity."

"Does that mean you intend to have someone of your choice manage our venture?"

"Not at all, I just want someone in place to oversee and direct the managers and to make sure the undertaking is proceeding as we have agreed. I don't want a manager I want a director. In fact I will appoint three people to carry out this function and call them my board of directors. One of these gentlemen will act as the president of the Company, one the treasurer and the last the secretary."

It was agreed. Upon their leaving the Prince stopped them and said, "By the way your name for the venture has to go. I prefer, 'The Hudson's Bay Company'." Of course Prince Rupert got his way on that too and so was born the first company incorporated in North America, the Hudson's Bay Company.

What do we see from all this? First there was an idea that could generate profit. Then there was money raised to put that idea into action. The people who provided the money (and the asset in the form of the trading rights) all were to share in the benefits. They were shareholders in the undertaking and their profits would be determined on the basis of the amount of their investment. Someone had to oversee the managers and insure that they were acting in the best interest of Prince Rupert and the other owners and as such they would direct the company's affairs through the managers. The directors served at the pleasure of the shareholders and would be remunerated at the whim of the shareholders.

So was born a corporation with investors, assets, business plan, managers, employees and a board of directors. The corporation had a president, treasurer and secretary. Two of those individuals signed pieces of paper which attested to the degree of ownership that a shareholder had in the venture. They called the recognition of their holding, share certificates.

Make Me an Offer
I Won't Refuse

Things were going well for the Hudson Bay Company Limited but young Wellesley, one of the original investors, was fascinated by what he had heard about the voyages of some foreigner by the name of Vasco di Gama. Apparently the chap had found a sea route to the Indies and the need to bring silks and spices overland through the rapacious Ottoman Empire was no longer mandatory. They could be brought by sea thus cutting out the Turks, Italians and all the other foreigners forcing up the prices of a good silk ruff and a pot of pepper. A company was once again being formed for just such voyages and the prospects as outlined in the prospectus[5] appealed to Wellesley's avarice. There was a minor problem in that the subscriptions for the new East India shares were on a cash basis and all Wellesley's funds were tied up in his Hudson Bay investment, which although profitable didn't have, in his mind, the potential of this new East India Company.

---

5   A prospectus is a document that outlines the use for the funds being raised. In present day application all new issues must be accompanied by a prospectus. In earlier times they were selling documents rather than informative.

Wellesley had heard that on most days a number of chaps got together in the City of London coffee shops near Bow Lane to buy and sell shares. If he could find a buyer for the Hudson Bay shares he could use the proceeds to purchase a piece of the hot new East India offering. At the Astralquid[6] Coffee House he encountered young George Baring who was known to trade in shares of foreign operating companies. George said he didn't know of anyone buying Hudson Bay these days as everyone was after the hot new East India issue which was certain to command a premium after issuance. However, seeing as George was a broker he would purchase from Wellesley his shareholding at a price. After a respectable period of time had been engaged in negotiating they struck a price at which each of them felt content. They both felt they had a bargain. Note that George Baring bought the shares from Wellesley. He, therefore, owned them and as such, was assuming some risk having bought the shares rather than sold them to someone on Wellesley's behalf he would therefore be called a broker, not an agent. Most people who call themselves stockbrokers today are actually agents acting on behalf of a client.

This was the start of stock markets as we know them. They were markets where people came to exchange shares when they felt that a new or different investment was more to their needs. Note again that Baring didn't sell the shares for Wellesley. He bought them for his own account from his client until such time as he could find a buyer. Up to this time the major trading of investments was done in Italy and Holland for 'Bills' which were the forerunners of today's bonds. Another innovation was that Wellesley, a forebear of the future Duke of Wellington, found it somewhat tiresome for a man of his distinction to be wandering around the streets of the City trying to off load some very common shares. When it came time to sell his East India shares he hired a young barrel boy named Cazenove (who's successors went on to found one of

---

6   Astralquid when translated into modern parlance is 'Starbucks'

England's premier investment houses) to go down to the City and find a buyer and it was from these barrel boys that the modern investment firm evolved.

It didn't take long for these barrel boys to realize that rushing from coffee house to wine bar to coffee house to find shares for sale or buyers for shares being offered was inefficient. The obvious answer was to get together at an agreed location in the morning and see if amongst the gathered crowd there was some possibility of clearing the items they held on their "book". Next, came the purpose designed building and they called it a stock exchange. Note it was not called an "early retirement exchange" or "get rich quick market", it was a place you went to exchange shares with others with the same intent.

There was however a problem. When the barrel boys, now stock brokers in the real sense, put up their funds to buy shares from clients they faced the issue of risk in holding the shares and the strain it put on their finances. At some point the broker would find it difficult to provide the money needed to cover the purchases from his clients and the money he did put up left him at risk if the market fell. The problem was liquidity. There was not enough money nor professionals in the market to assure that there would always be someone to buy from or sell to. The answer was simple. Keep the trading function for the professionals as they would be the only ones to be able to execute a trade but allow the public into the market place to act as a buffer. If the public could be convinced that they could buy and sell shares and make a profit they would come in droves. These were not people involved in investing, but people pursuing the quick buck from capital gain.

Once the public entered the market place there would be a pool of money to buy the shares the broker wanted to off load and a similar pool of shares of shares available to buy when necessary to fill an investors order.

Admittedly, to fill a large order the broker might have to pay increasing prices to fill his entire order but that cost could be passed on to his client. The same applied to a disposition of shares. An investor's order to sell could be dribbled out into the hands of speculators with some downward pressure on prices but again the client could bear the cost to be rid of what he or she no longer considered appropriate.

Granny, where do shares come from?

In bygone years some mothers would dread the day when an off-spring would wonder into the room and ask the question "where do babies come from?" and they therefore prepared in advance. The question grandmothers will have to answer is almost as important, "Granny, where do shares come from?" I intend to prepare Granny for that eventuality.

There are four sources of shares for the public to purchase:

> The Private Placement. This is an issue of shares from the treasury of a company offered to a limited number of sophisticated investors and which will not be immediately tradable on an exchange. The Hudson Bay issue you saw was one such Private Placement.

> The Initial Primary Offering or IPO. These are shares that arise from the company's treasury or existing shareholders or both. The shares that were issued as a Private Placement might now be offered by some investors to the public along with the new treasury

shares. This is the first time the shares are to be offered to the public.

The Treasury Issue. When a company finds itself in need of funding it can borrow the money through issuing IOU's also known as bonds or debentures, obtain funding from a bank or sell a portion of itself to the public. It is this latter event that provides new shares to be held by the public.

The Secondary Issue. Original founders of a company or large shareholders decide, for whatever reason, that they want to own fewer shares of the company and therefore offer a portion or all their holding to the market.

As you saw in the previous chapter with the formation of the Hudson Bay Company the promoters of the venture went around to people and asked them to subscribe for shares. This would be in current parlance a 'private placement' in that shares were sold to investors privately by the company raising the funds. These are still done today in speculative ventures at the early establishment of an enterprise. Agent- vendors may call on non-related parties to buy shares and if they do so they will receive an agent's fee. In modern times the vendor will provide a document outlining the terms of the issue along with the subscription form. In this way the investor will know what it is he or she is financing and under what terms. What happens when someone wants to raise the funds necessary to pay for a pipeline or railroad extending across Canada? Obviously you can't just stroll down to the gentlemen's club and ask if a number of the chaps can pony up two or three billion dollars for the new venture. The answer is the public. Perhaps there are enough patriotic and avaricious citizens out there in this great country to underwrite the new asset. And so was born the 'Initial Public

Offering' or IPO as it so casually referred to today. These are always accompanied by a prospectus which, as the name implies, shows the 'prospects' for the venture. These documents can be daunting although the market regulators have attempted to bring these down to a level comprehensible to most financial workers. However, when these are presented to a layman with no financial training, they pose difficulties. At this point I should point out that some people have allowed the lines between accounting and finance to become blurred. Accounting as the name implies involves the counting of money. Finance is bringing money to the best suited venture and the husbanding of that resource. They are two different fields which some neophytes don't distinguish. An accountant could no sooner raise the funding for a transcontinental pipeline than a financier could determine if the funds had been properly spent.

Because a prospectus is a dry, legal document it is seldom read by laymen and I fear not as often as it should be by the stock salesmen offering you the new issue. My idea of hell would be to be imprisoned in a library having to read a dozen prospecti a day for my daily bread in perpetuity. If these documents are so daunting then why should they exist? They exist because they are the birth certificates of the new issue.

After The Private Placement

If the company issues a private placement that does not imply that the shares are immediately tradable on the stock exchange. In fact, the company may not have a listing on an exchange. As well, private placement shares usually have a restriction on them as to when the original purchaser can sell them on an exchange, often four months or more. So if you were to be considered a sophisticated investor, you might buy a portion of a private placement well aware that there is no market for the shares and you are stuck with them for a pre-defined hold period or only able to sell them privately.

Of course, the question is where do these come from and why would anyone buy them. Let's suppose that your niece, Ariadne, has invented a device to test whether a driver's testosterone level was too high for him to handle a car for fear of road rage. "Test Test" the private company she has set up to produce and sell this device, needs start-up capital. Who better to go to than her nearest and dearest 50 friends[7] and relatives? Ariadne uses the funds to further

---

7   In most jurisdictions there is a limit as to the number of people that can be solicited for a private placement thus preventing it from becoming a "public issue".

advance her device and interests the Vulture Venture Fund in the outlook for this device. That fund, Vulture Venture Fund, provides financing to continue development, prepare a prospectus for an Initial Public Offering (IPO) and markets the shares to investors. The existence of the prospectus does not necessarily mean that the shares will be trading on an exchange. They could be "unlisted" and as such change hands privately or trade "over the counter". This is the typical unlisted public issue. If they trade over the counter it means you are back to some barrel boy willing to either buy or sell at some price and then offer to the public.

If the company can meet some exchange's listing requirements whether it be in Frankfurt, New York, London or Toronto, to name but a few, the shares will be posted for trading. This means that there will be shares offered for sale and bids made to buy the company's shares noted at the exchange. Because the listing process required the disclosure of all the company's pertinent information, buying and selling a listed share allows for a greater degree of confidence of what the value of the share might be. When there is a general agreement as to the worth of the company and its shares, there is usually a minimal difference in the offering price of the shares and the price being bid i.e. what someone will pay.

The first advice here is that irrespective of the fact that Ariadne is a PhD physicist with an MBA you should not participate in hers or anyone else's private placement. The vendors of these will tell you of the very high possible rewards from owning these shares and they are right. But with great reward comes great risk which is why they are marketed to "sophisticated investors". Even at the IPO stage, as much as you may love your niece, it is better to avoid these shares. You may ask is there a time when they can be bought and the answer is, yes. That time is when the company announces that they are instituting a dividend program. In other words they are going to pay you for being a partial owner of the company.

So there is the gestation process for a share of stock, shareholding or whatever you want to call it. As you've seen a company is formed, and at the outset there will be shares sold or given in exchange for some asset. These shares are privately held and funds can be raised by selling, in a very restricted manner, shares to other private investors. When the company has achieved a patina of viability the owners of the company will apply for an exchange listing thus providing their shareholders a broader market in which to dispose of shares and investors interested in the company an arena in which to buy the stock. Taking an idea from its inception to a full-fledged company is much like the zygote to full grown fetus process. What happens after the IPO is like the teenage years and then will come the corporate adulthood with dividends and all the trappings of respectability. But like all living things there is an end. Companies like cars or appliances have a limited period of usefulness. Where is the Studebaker Car Company? Or National Lead? Remember Nortel? All these companies were important and profitable at one time then they became irrelevant, they then died.

The IPO

There it is on the front page of the financial papers, Almost Effective Therapeutics is considering "going public". In other words the company is going to issue shares to the investing public from its treasury, an Initial Public Offering or IPO. What is not highlighted is that the original insiders of the company are going to sell a portion of their holdings along with the treasury shares. The debate is raging in the financial journals as to what the issue price will be. If the underwriters price it too high the issue might not be fully subscribed, too low and the company's treasury will receive less than it should. What is the value of the shares of a company developing an elixir that will at best prevent divorce and at worst end custody battles? Field trials have indicated that divorce rates for octogenarians taking the elixir were well below those of thirty year olds and custody battles over pets in the thirty year old group using the formula well below that of disputes over children. This could be a winner.

The salesmen for the underwriter are calling their most remunerative institutional clients offering the new issue but warning them that the amount that they subscribe for may be cut back if the issue is oversubscribed.

What does this mean to you? Note that, in the first instance, the issue is being offered to institutions such as pension and mutual funds, the big buyers. For the underwriter this makes her job easier as she has to pitch fewer clients, but what about you and the issuing company? Both would like to see a broader distribution of the shares to provide a stable market. That is not the underwriter's concern. The underwriter wants to sell the issue quickly and see a "bounce" in the share price when trading begins, the reason being that the buyers will be happy to see their shares open for trading at a price higher than they paid for them. Also, it is likely that the underwriters did not sell all the shares being offered but kept a portion for themselves to dispose of in the aftermarket when trading begins at hopefully a price higher than issue.

What does it mean to the underwriter? The underwriter is in the business to make money. She may not see this underwriting client ever again, although there is a tradition that the client should return to the last broker she used for an issue. The underwriting firm acting in its brokerage function will continue to work with the buyers of the shares on a daily basis doing their investment business. It is obvious that the underwriter's allegiance lies with the "street", the investors. But note that the highest level of allegiance is with the largest clients. The underwriter will try to underprice the issue.

What does it mean to the institutional investor? She will scramble to get as much of the issue as possible and oversubscribe. She knows that the issue will be underpriced and the price will bounce when cleared for public trading as those who could not get a piece of the issue scramble into the market to buy some.

What is the result? There were roughly 7,100 new issues done between 1998 and 2008. The performance of that group was that on average their share prices advanced 18 percent from issue price within three days after issue and were down 20 percent three years after issue. Remembering that the underwriter will first approach the professionals to take advantage of the "free money", if she calls you about the issue it probably means that the professionals have already turned it down.

Is this Right Warranted?

There was a time, not so very long ago, when corporate managements were very respectful of the people who made their position and salaries possible – the shareholders. The shareholders took all the risk at the private placement and IPO stages therefore should they not be shown some consideration in future financings?

Up until the 1990's the existing shareholders were believed by management to be privileged. As a result if new share issues were being contemplated the existing shareholders were considered to have the first right of refusal to buy the new issue of shares. This very fair and sensible idea was accomplished by the issue to existing shareholders of "rights" to buy soon to be issued new shares at a fixed price, usually at a discount from current market prices. The rights were issued in proportion to the number of shares held by the existing shareholder.

These *rights* were usually immediately listed for trading on the same exchange as the shares themselves. If the *right* entitled the shareholder to buy at $9.90 from the corporate treasury a share that was currently priced at $10.00 on the exchange the *right* became valuable as it could be sold to a speculator wanting to own the $10.00 share but only having to pay $9.90 if purchased from the corporate treasury with a *right*. The recipient of the *right* could make the decision whether to buy the new issue or abstain by selling the *right*. What could fairer?

The use of *rights* was problematic. Consider that the corporation had to decide on an issue price for the shares that would not be too dilutive (but even then the dilution was occurring to the existing shareholders). However the price had to be attractive enough that all the *rights* would be exercised. If all the *rights* were not exercised the company would not achieve its financing goals.

It was at this juncture that "back stopping" was utilized wherein a group would guarantee to obtain and exercise any rights that may not otherwise be executed. As a result most rights issues were a success.

Think of the logic. Who better to sell a new issue of shares to than existing shareholders who are currently aware of the company's circumstance and would want to see any dilution benefit themselves rather than some parvenus?

Rights issues were killed off by their costs and the uncertainty of raising all the capital needed if there was no backstopping. The advent of real underwriting where a broker bought the entire new issue and parceled it out to other brokers and the public was the coup de grace. Will they ever return? It depends on whether you believe in altruism and honesty. Personally, I doubt that this very fair type of share issue will return.

A security that has replaced the rights is the warrant. This security has some of the same logic as the rights issue. A warrant is a certificate issued as attached to a new issue security. Thus when you buy the new issue of Last Chance Mines it may consist of a share and a warrant with the package priced at $1.00. When you pay your broker you are given two pieces of papers (actually two electronic entries in your account) one being the share certificate of Last Chance Mines and the other being a warrant that allows you to buy more shares at a pre-set price from the treasury over a defined period of time. Typically, with the Last Chance Mining shares trading at let's say $1.00 the company announces that it will issue one million new shares with a warrant attached to each share that will allow the holder to purchase of a further share from the treasury at $1.50 for a period of two years. The warrant is usually posted for trading on an exchange when issued. The new shares with warrant attached are priced at $1.00 for the package. This seems quite fair as the new shareholder is taking some risk and why should she not be rewarded. If the funds raised increase the value of the company and its share price to over $1.50, then the warrant becomes valuable. If the shares trade at $2.00 then the warrant holder has the option of buying shares from the treasury at $1.50 with her warrant and selling them into the marketplace at $2.00 for a profit of $0.50 per share. The speculators will also recognize that there is a benefit of buying the shares from the treasury at $1.50 rather than at the $2.00 exchange offered price and thus bid up the price of the warrants to eliminate the price advantage. The warrant holder therefore has two avenues of profit the first as above she exercises her warrant to buy cheap shares and sells those on the exchange or she can sell her warrant for something approaching $0.50 each.

From the corporation's view the warrants are a liability. Think of the situation wherein the above example Last Chance Mining uses the million dollars to fund a drilling program which locates a billion dollar orebody. With 100 million shares outstanding the value of the shares is well beyond $1.50 a share and more likely closer to $10 (billion dollar asset divided by 100 million shares). However because of the existence of the warrants the company is forced to sell shares at $1.50 each. You may well ask why the company would choose to issue warrants.

The warrants are an inducement to buy the new issue of treasury shares. In the above example the company would not be able to sell a new issue at $1.00 per share when the speculator had the option of buying the same share on the exchange at $1.00. Therefore by adding the warrant to the package the company provides an incentive to bring in new buyers.

Recently there have been issues of warrants as separate entities that is they are not attached to a share. The corporation sells the warrants to the public and then hopes that forthcoming events will push the share price higher thus encouraging the exercise of the warrants. In the above example Last Chance Mines could have sold a million warrants at a price of $0.05 per warrant exercisable to buy the company shares for $1.00 for five years.

From the speculators point of view if he believes the shares will go beyond $1.50 then has two ways to approach that expectation. The first is to buy the existing shares at $1.00 each and sell them in a years' time at say $1.50 or more. His total cost to hold a share for a year is the dollar he put up plus the $0.05 in interest costs for tying up his capital for a year for a total of $1.05. His other alternative is to buy a warrant for $0.05 and exercise it when the shares are trading at $1.50. His purchase cost for the shares by exercising the warrant is $1.00 per share and his cost of the warrant of $0.05 for a total of $1.05. His interest cost to hold the $0.05 warrant is negligible. In the first case the return to the speculator is 43 percent ($0.45/$1.05). In the using the warrant the speculator makes $0.45 when buying the share for a dollar and selling it for $1.50 a profit of $0.45(after deducting the cost of the warrant) on an investment of $0.05 or 900 percent.

You may well ask why would anyone buy the shares when the warrant offers a much more lucrative potential outcome? The answer is that if the during the 5 year life of the warrant the shares never trade over the $1.00 exercise price the warrant will expire worthless. After the 5 years have ended the shareholder still has something of value, the shares.

Not the Shares Granny, the Other Security!

Ah yes, if little Penelope has had her nose in the business section she has seen the term "bond". Not being old enough to enjoy spy novels she will not associate this "bond" with 007 but assume that there is some connection to the financial markets.

I should warn you that the use of the term "bond" is very sloppy. We all know what a skirt or dress is but what is an outfit? What the outfit is to fashion, the bond is to financial markets. First off there are two types of bonds, corporate and government.

When you were in school it is likely that you read Shakespeare's "the Merchant of Venice". As well as probably being the English language's first feminist play in that the heroine/hero saves the day, it was the earliest English drama involving a bond or promissory note. The issue was a loan document that ended up in the hands of Shylock who was also a shylock. Seeing as we don't know the terms of the loan we can't be sure if it was a "note" or a "bond".

The term "bond" arises from the fact that if you borrow money from someone you are "bound" to repay them and hence issue your "bond" to do so. The most commonly referred to is the government bond. This is an IOU issued by a government to the public.

Originally these were issued by governments to finance some public works like a road, dam or building. Then came along what has always been the great rot in government, the "national emergency". This event is used to debase every facet of good and democratic government. In Canada income tax and federal government borrowing for other than capital projects was adopted in 1917 so that Canadians could finance the great patriotic slaughter of its youth. But as well as providing guns, taxation made the country's capital relevant. That relevance stems from the "Golden Rule" which is that he who has the gold, rules, and Ottawa was now collecting the gold in the form of taxes and hence being able to rule the provinces. When the war ended there was a serious mountain of debt but it was not offset by a lot of infrastructure generating revenue to pay for the debt. Then came the next, in the politicians' eyes, "national emergency" that of getting re-elected and so bribing the electorate with current borrowings to provide outlandish benefits, (think of Greece). Needless to say the world is awash with government bonds.

Exactly what is this bond, you may ask. It is a piece of paper issued by a borrower stating how much he has borrowed from you, when he will repay, what amount of interest he will pay and when he will pay it. As well the borrower states what assets he is pledging as payment should he default and not pay the principal when due. As you saw in Shakespeare's times the issuers of this kind of paper were individuals. Money was borrowed to finance such things as a trading expedition and a note or bond issued to attest to that. Then it evolved that groups of individuals who had founded a corporation needed to borrow, and hence came the corporate bond. There are in fact two bond markets; the government and the corporate. A government bond is backed by the ability of the government to tax without restraint. Corporate bonds were originally secured by an asset in the same way your mortgage is secured by your house. If the debtor failed to pay the creditor would seize the asset backing the bond. Current practice is for the corporate debenture to be backed by the company's ability to pay – not a specific asset. If a forest products company wishes to build a new paper mill it doesn't borrow money backed by a bond allowing the seizure of the new mill but by the full good faith of the corporation to pay both its interest and the amount borrowed (principal) when due. This piece of paper is more correctly referred to as a "debenture". If the borrower fails to pay either his interest or principal the debenture holders will take court action to either force the payment or seize sufficient of the corporate assets in payment.

The corporate bond market was the first to evolve as individuals were in enterprise long before national or local governments began to provide infrastructure. Even the issue that led to the insolvency of the Medici family of Florence, a loan to Henry IV of England, was in fact a personal loan and lead to a great distaste to the lending of money to rulers of any country.

Return of or on Capital?

Every real investment is based on the annuity model. Let's go back to Sophia and Dimitri. Sophia has built up some savings which she calls her "capital". It is sitting in Athens with the banker, Onassis, who pays her ten percent per year to leave her funds with him. However, what she would like to do is expand the farming operation and a new goat would be part of that expansion. In looking around the market she spots a likely candidate.

"How much milk does she produce?" asks Sophia.

"About a liter a week."

"And kids?"

"So far a couple per year."

"How much do you want for her?"

"10 drachmas."

At this point Sophia sits down with her abacus and does some calculations. She concludes that she can sell the two kids for about half a drachma a piece and the milk should fetch about a drachma per year. So all in, she can expect to make two drachmas per year from this goat, her return on investment. The goat will last about six years so in total she will make 12 drachmas from the goat over the life of the investment. However, before she plunks her money down, the 10 drachmas, she has to figure her costs. She pays nothing to feed the goat as it forages so there is only one other cost to factor in and that is her cost of capital. Remember she is going to have to go to Onassis and withdraw 10 drachmas from her account. That means she will have to give up 1.0 drachmas in interest every year (10 drachmas X 10 percent = 1.0 drachmas) for six years for a total of 6.0 drachmas. Sophia has to recover her investment in the goat which is the cost of the money she had to put up to buy it before she makes a profit. She knows she is going to make the 2 drachmas per year she calculated and this has to cover all her costs, which is her cost of capital at 1.0 drachmas per year. Remember that Sophia is foregoing 1.0 drachmas a year in interest that she would have made had she left her money with Onassis. So her real earnings from the goat annually are 1.0 drachmas per year (sales of 2 drachmas per year minus cost of capital of 1.0 drachmas per year giving 1.0 drachmas). If the goat is going to net her 1.0 drachmas for 6 years, after which it will die with no salvage value, the most she can afford to pay for it is 6.0 drachmas (6 X1.0 = 6.0). The purchase of the new goat does not make business sense until her return on capital is higher than what she makes with the banker and that can only happen if she pays less than 6.0 drachmas or can earn more through higher milk and kid prices. At the end of 6 years she must have in hand the original investment (10 drachmas) and the interest she would have earned (6 drachmas) for a total of 16 drachmas.

When you put up your money as an investment in a security you should look at whether or not it covers your cost of capital and will it return your investment at the end of your period of investment. If someone were to offer you a mining stock for $2.00 per share in a mine that had two years of life left but paid dividends of $1.00 per year you could expect over the life of the investment, 2 years, to make $2.00 (ignoring taxes) for an investment you paid $2.00 for. You have traded dollars as the saying goes, and made nothing for your investment. If the money you used to buy the mining share came from your bank that was paying you three percent interest per year you would have had to give up two years of interest payment ($2.00 X 3 percent = $0.06 per year) so you would have in fact lost money on the deal as your dividends at $2.00 are not equal to your total cost of the investment $2.12 ($2.00 capital or purchase cost plus foregone interest of $0.06 per year).

An investment in bonds or debentures makes that calculation simpler as you put up your investment, usually $1,000 per bond, receive interest for a set period and then have your $1,000 returned to you. Looking at the share market is not as simple. If you purchased a share of the Bank of Montreal at $50.00 and you received from the Bank $2.80 in dividends per year you would have a return on your investment of 5.6 percent. If you decided to hold the shares for 5 years as you were going to then use the funds for a cruise, what would your return be if the shares were now selling at $48.00 or $60.00?

If you sold for $48.00 per share after 5 years your total return would be $14.00 from dividends (5 X $2.80 = $14.00) minus the $2.00 per share you lost on the sale of the share for a total of $12.00 over 5 years or 4.8 percent per year. On the basis of a $60.00 sale and using the methodology below, you made 9.6 percent per year. As you can see planning for a financial event, such as paying for a cruise, forces you to make assumptions about the future if you own shares. **You cannot foretell the price of a share at the time you wish to sell it.**

RETURN ON INVESTMENT

Purchase one share Bank of Montreal	$50.00
Dividends received over 5 years (5 X $2.80)	$14.00
Sale of Bank of Montreal share	$48.00
Total Return = Sale - Purchase + income received = $50.00 - $48.00 + $14.00	$12.00
Percentage return over 5 years = $12.00/$50.00	24%
Simple percentage per year = 24%/5years	4.8%

Alternatively your nephew has convinced you that "Click Technologies" is the company of the future and you put up $50.00 per share to buy a position. The shares pay no dividend so how much do they have to appreciate over five years to give you the same return you expected from the Bank of Montreal? Obviously, looking at total return to be equivalent to holding the Bank of Montreal and selling at $48.00 and receiving $14 in dividends you would have to realize $62 per share for "Click" (24 percent increase) to equal what you would have made by just holding your bank of Montreal. If the Bank of Montreal were to be sold at $60.00 then Click Technologies would have to be priced at $74 per share in five years to give you the equivalent price. Which would you rather have; the almost certain $2.80 per year dividend and then whatever you can get for the bank shares or hope for a price increase of almost 50 percent in the technology shares?

Real annuities, which are where we all eventually end up, pay you a portion of your capital every year and interest on what is left. In the real world if you had a 20 or so years to live and you bought a $100,000 annuity you could expect to receive about $6,000 per year some of which would be capital and some interest and at the end of the twenty years your investment would have been returned to you interest paid and the annuity ended. You want the same thing from investing unless of course you are a speculator. A classic story of the investor versus the speculator concerned Bernard Baruch and Jay Pierpont Morgan.

At the turn of the 19th century three prospectors in Alaska had found what appeared to be a mountain of copper near the Kennecott Glacier in Alaska. The property was in a remote location and would therefore require immense amounts of capital to develop. The prospectors engaged Mr. Baruch to find them the financing as he was at the time a swashbuckling young capitalist and the darling of Wall Street. Baruch knew that the kind of funds he would need for the project had to come from deep pockets and the deepest in America belonged to J.P. Morgan. After three weeks and much favor trading a meeting was arranged in Mr. Morgan's offices. It went as follows.

"Good morning Mr. Morgan."

"Good morning Mr. Baruch."

"Sir, I have in Alaska one of the best gambles you can ever take in the copper market."

"Good day Mr. Baruch."

"Sir, can I not tell you of the enormity of this venture?"

"No sir. I invest I do not gamble, good day."

The project did proceed with funding from the Guggenheim interests. As a result of that speculation the Guggenheims obtained a vast fortune from the Kennecott Mine that eventually over time they managed to speculate away. Whereas, J. P. Morgan provided the capital in 1907 to save the US government from financial collapse.

You, I hope are an investor not a speculator. If you are a speculator put this book down.

I Want To Get Paid By You, Just You Nobody Else Will Do

Actually that is a paraphrase of an old Marilyn Munroe song where "paid" has been substituted for "loved". For the investor getting paid is more rewarding than being loved. Previously we have talked about getting paid when you loan money to a corporation or a government. What happens if you buy a piece of a business?

What if instead of loaning money to your nephew to start his bicycle courier business you offer to partner with him. You are into a whole new realm of investing. Because you know little of the bike courier business you choose to be a silent partner. You have purchased a 50 percent interest in the business and have a document attesting to that. Let's say your nephew is brilliant and the business succeeds wildly. At the end of the first year he announces that the business has made a net profit of $5,000. He of course has to split this with you the other 50 percent partner. As the years go by you advise your nephew to incorporate so as to relieve you both of liability inherent in a partnership[8] should one of the couriers cause an accident. After a few years the company has become extremely profitable with $100,000 per year in earnings now the norm. Your nephew at this point in time decides that rather than paying out half the earnings to auntie, that lavish new offices are in order as well as glamorous new bike helmets specially made emblazoned with the company logo. Nephew is also contemplating investing the earnings in a number of trucks to serve coffee and snacks to bikers and other street workers.

You now recognize that there will no longer be distributions of your company's earnings and that expenditures and investment of questionable validity are being undertaken. You ask your nephew to arrange a shareholder's and director's meeting to discuss these matters. Seeing as at that meeting the directors (you and your nephew) cannot agree to the payment of the earnings to the shareholders (a dividend) the meeting is adjourned and you sell your interest back to your nephew for a negotiated price.

What you have just seen is a microcosm of the investment market generally. When you put up your money it was to finance a bicycle courier business with the hope that it would be profitable and like Sophia's goats provide you the benefits of that profitability in perpetuity. You do not see your nephew as an investment guru being able to discover great possibilities in street level business. Your nephew is a brilliant bike courier and couriering strategist. You are as much of an investment guru as he is in that you chose to invest in his business sensing that it would be a success.

---

8   In a partnership all the partners are responsible for all the liabilities of the partnership irrespective of the extent to which they participate. In an adverse legal situation the plaintiffs will pursue all the partners to the extent they can pay. In a corporate structure you are liable for the 'par' value of the share you own. Most shares today are issued with no par value hence the sometimes seen NPV (No Par Value) designation after a shares description.

In the investment markets you can buy a piece of a company in the form of a shareholding. At the end of the year you would expect that the directors would know how much money the company made and pay that out to the owners i.e. shareholders. That seldom occurs and you are well intentioned to ask why not.

Here is another quote, "How do I pay thee? Let me count the ways" again a paraphrase of "How do I love thee? Let me count the ways". Let see about getting paid for your investments.

Getting the Right Cut

Wives and mothers in the past have walked into supermarkets and been confronted with a meat cooler full of a variety of choices of pieces of the steer. There's rump roast, sirloin, steaks, ribs and all sorts of offal to name a few. For the woman of the house that part was easy. She knew who she was feeding and what would be needed. But what about the lady who walks into the stock market and sees on offer common shares, preferred shares, convertible shares and debentures, debentures, and bonds and let's not even mention the mutual and exchange traded funds which one could liken to sausages. Thankfully they are all cuts off one animal, the corporation. The woman has to make choices from the offerings to feed her investment plan. There is the question of freshness and quality. You don't just squeeze the common shares to see if they're firm. Do the debentures seem a little tired? Does the new issue of shares being offered have that three day old smell of fish and is to be avoided? If everybody is buying lobsters is it not better to consider a steak for tonight? On the other hand maybe there is a glut of lobsters and what one is seeing is a true bargain on offer rather than a shopping fad.

In the past, the male member of the family walked into the shares market and could spot the dodgy gas play as quickly as his mate could avoid soggy lettuce in the supermarket. However, take that same man into the supermarket and ask him to pick out the fresh fish from the stale and he would be lost. However, with a little coaching we could soon teach him the distinguishing features between fresh and stale. So let's do some coaching. Let's do that for the mistress of the house with regard to investments.

The products that are shown on the shelves in the stock market are all cuts from the same body. The source is the corporate body and there many ways you can participate in the products derived from this product as there are many cuts of a steer.

We'll start with the most common cut from the corporate steer the, the common share. As you saw, this originated when a number of partners pooled their funds to invest in a scheme which could provide a profitable outcome. A corporate beast was created and cut up into pieces called shares. To avoid the liabilities associated with partnerships, where the partners are liable for each other's liabilities in the venture, the investor chose to follow a limited liability form of structure called the company. If this is a new venture, how do the investors know what they are putting their money into?

They are provided with a document called a prospectus. This outlines what the company's business will be, how it will be conducted and some 'pro forma' financial statements. These forward looking documents are fraught with danger as no one can foretell the future and the pro forma statements are always issued with a warning. However, the pro formas have to be realistic and in tune with what a 'prudent man'[9] would assume. The prospectus will also name the directors of the new venture. This is of considerable importance as you might be concerned if the board contained a roster of names such as Ponzi, Madoff, Stanford, and Ebbers. These are extremes but if on the other hand you see the names of people who have been

---

9   The 'prudent man' denomination in the investment industry is a corner stone in that actions taken by a person dealing with the investors funds cannot be reckless.

immensely successful and of high integrity then you have some confidence that the venture is honest and of some potential.

Having read the prospectus what do you know? Who the supporters or promoters are and what are their intentions. If this is such a good deal why are they offering a piece of it to you? Is this yesterday's fish? It may just be. There is a good rule to adopt:

Never buy what others want to sell:

Buy what you want to own

When I was a partner at a highly successful boutique investment firm, the assets of which were the partners capabilities, I would often hear our senior partner moaning when considering the future, 'What are we to do? Turn off the lights and give the keys to the landlord?' Actually that would have been the honorable thing to do but the avaricious thing to do was have an Initial Private Offering (IPO) of shares to the public so that we, the partners, had somebody to sell to at prices far inflated from the values[10] that we did business amongst ourselves. In recent years you have seen the avaricious approach as brokers and investment counsel firms have sold themselves to the public at highly inflated prices without acknowledging that the true assets of the firm were the people who toiled there and would someday be gone. There was also the issue of the big fat bonuses that are to be paid before the shareholders participate[11]. This is so truly yesterday's fish. Would you pay the

---

10   The investment firms used to buy and sell shares to the participants in the firm at 'book value', in other words at the intrinsic cash value of the enterprise (assets – liabilities). This was very conservative and gave no value to the ongoing name value or established business. However, recognizing that the assets of the firm where the people who rode up and down the elevator everyday it was realistic. When they sold their firms to the banks and public it was at three and four time's book value.

11   Lehman Brothers after going from a private partnership to public company only paid bonuses to employees, never dividends to the shareholders.

same price for Warren Buffet's firm, Berkshire Hathaway, after he leaves voluntarily or involuntarily?

The IPO is the "Initial Public Offering" of a company's shares and represents their first entry to the market. Before even considering the price look at the reason for the issue. At the time of this writing the market has seen the consideration of IPO's for everything from ski hills to airlines (which as Warren Buffet declared were the greatest destroyer of capital the 21st century had ever seen). Why are the current owners so generous as to offer you these delicacies? Let's think about it for a moment. A ski hill anywhere is going to be faced with global warming. That is going to lead to a shorter season and hence lower earnings. The ski hill was the remnant of a real estate development anchored to the resort. Once the real estate had been completely sold there was little profit generating potential left in the remaining ski hill. Better to blow it off to the public.

The airline had a monopoly situation as a result of an un-expandable airport franchise. It was the only airline flying from a downtown airport. All its competitors had to fly from the suburbs. In spite of this the company could not report a profitable year. It could hope for one though. If the privileged landing rights are offered to competitors as well, what is the airline worth? Not much. Better, in the vendor's mind that the public should own it rather than the founder.

What I have been talking about is a new share issue in an untried venture where there is little history to refer to other than at best the past 5 years performance of the enterprise as shown in the prospectus. Then there is the pricing problem. There would have been some negotiating between the company whose shares are being sold and the investment syndicate offering them for sale. Obviously, the company wishes to maximize the value of the shares they are selling while the syndicate selling the shares wishes to see as low a price as possible to make the shares appealing to the buyers. If the pricing is too high the dealer will be left with shares to return to the owners or forced to sell them at a loss. In the latter case this would depress the market share price and the new investor would be displeased with the dealer. From a pricing point of view the investor is getting a reasonable offer.

The other method of selling shares for companies is on a "bought deal" basis. In this case the vendor (the issuing company) will agree with a purchaser (the investment, dealer, broker) as to a price and the purchaser will do his utmost to sell the paper. Whatever is not sold is held by the purchaser/broker or syndicate or sold at a loss. In this instance the investment dealer is truly acting as a "broker" in that he is buying for his own account from the company treasury and selling at his own risk.

When you buy investments from an initial public offering, they can be compared to produce fresh from the farm unlike buying in the stock exchange where the shares are pre-owned and being sold off by someone who believes that the price is beyond fair value. You can almost compare the process as buying from the farmer and then preserving the product for resale, sort of like canned tomatoes sold in the winter when fresh are no longer available. After an IPO the company may find reasons to go to the markets again to raise money. When a corporation is expanding faster than it can generate cash flow to finance that growth it must either borrow money or sell off part of the ownership. If the public is to be the source of those funds then either a share or debt issue must be undertaken.

A very similar issue to the IPO I showed you is the secondary offering. This arises when the controlling shareholder of a company or founder decides that it is time to leave or that the business has lost its shine. Better to blow off his position in the shares to the public and seek greener pastures. Again the question arises. 'If this is so good why is he offering it to me?' Because of this question secondary offerings are very difficult to sell. The other problem for secondary offerings is that they depress the market. Once the whiff of the likelihood of the offering becomes apparent, investor who might have bought the shares at the current price withdraw their bids knowing that a glut of stock is about to hit the market. It is this depressing of the price that leads students of investing to believe that markets are efficient in that increased supply leads to lower pricing.

You now have the answer to the granddaughter's question of "where do shares common from", but what if there are no initial public offerings, new subsequent issues and no secondary distributions going on and you still want shares in a particular company. You're going to have to go for pre-owned.

If you decide to do your own shopping realize that there is a one in four chance that your basket of purchases will outperform the stock market's 6 percent average annual return. If you don't feel that confident in your investing capabilities then take advantage of what technology has brought to the investor.

What's it Worth?

The buying of a share involves a purchase price. Who determines that price? Within the great unwashed mass of the market place someone will offer to buy a share at a price which is the highest the exchange has listed at the time. That is the bid price. There is as well someone willing to sell at the lowest price which constitutes the offer. These are merely numbers in that they do not necessarily reflect the underlying value of the share. When the two prices coincide a transaction takes place which in England's Edwardian time was described as a bargain. This was because both parties, buyer and seller, had achieved the prices they wanted. But again the question arises, "Was that price the value of the share?"

Nobody really knows which is why there are speculators buying and selling shares. The buyer hopes the share is underpriced with respect to value while the seller believes that she has "beat" the market by selling an overpriced share. This then begs the question, "Can you ascribe a value to a share?" yes.

Book Value: The most basic value is "book value". A corporation has an accounting form known as a balance sheet on which the left side records all of the company's assets while the right side its liabilities. Obviously deducting the value of the liabilities from the assets should leave a positive number[12] which is the net asset value. That number divided by the number of shares outstanding is the book value per share. It would seem intuitive that the share price should reflect this value but as always there are problems with valuations.

When a company makes an expenditure to develop software or drill an oil field the values of the asset produced by that expenditure is the amount that was spent. So if "Soft Shell" spent $10 million to develop a software package that would fetch $100 million if sold, the balance sheet will show only a $10 million valuation for the product. If you calculated the book value for "Soft Shell" by subtracting the liabilities from the assets your number would be technically correct but understate the company's true worth by $90 million.

On the other hand the old Kodak Company had a book value reflecting its holding of patents and facilities to manufacture and process film. What are those worth in an age of digital photography?

Once past the dilemma of assigning book value how would one price it? Should the share price equal the book value? Book value does not determine the company's ability to generate profit and hence pay you your quarterly dividend. All it tells you is the best approximation of the value of the net assets. It is up to company management to use those in such a way as to generate a profit and send you a cheque. But wait a minute, we just mentioned profitability. Is there a valuation method based on profits? Yes.

---

12 If the liabilities exceed the assets the company is technically bankrupt.

Price Earnings P/E: When investors talk about bonds and notes they compare them on the basis of yield which is the amount received by the investor divided by the price of the instrument. So the Mammoth Corporation bond yield is:

Yield $=$ interest received / cost of bond $=$ $50/$1000 $=$ 5%

That seems simple and straight forward but for reasons I have never been able to fathom the equity or stock trading people could not accept that presentation and insisted on what they call the price earnings ratio which is the share price divided by the earnings. So the Mammoth Corporation price earnings ratio based on that same information is:

PE $=$ share price / earnings per share $=$ $1000/$50 $=$ 20

So if the Mammoth Corporation shares were trading at $1000 per share and the company had earned $50 per share last year the price earnings ratio or P/E would be 20. **As you can see the P/E is just the yield calculation upside down**. That all seems simple enough except for the question of what are the earnings? It brings to mind the tale of businessman hiring a new accountant. He asked the first applicant, "Given these numbers what would your answer be based on?" The applicant replied "The accrual method." The second applicant replied to the same question, "The cash method." The third applicant replied, "My answer would be based on what you wanted them to be." The third applicant obviously was hired. So it is with corporate accounting. The final numbers can be whatever the corporation wants them to be, within reason. I experienced an example of this when as a mining analyst I viewed the Noranda Mining earnings and noted that every year they increased 11 percent irrespective of the performance of metal markets which are the driver of mining earnings. What I soon discovered was that by the judiciously including or excluding the earnings of subsidiaries and the choosing of when to charge exploration and other expenses the earnings could be kept to that magic 11 percent number.

Because of the price-earnings concept the level of earnings have a large influence on the share price. What management does not want the investors to see is erratic or surprising earnings. As a result reported earnings are massaged. To get around this the analyst and investor communities prefer to look at - EBITDA. That translated into English is **E**arnings **B**efore **I**nterest **T**axes **D**epreciation and **A**mortization. This sprung from the loins of a much cruder number - Operating Cash Flow. Operating cash flow was simply calculated by deducting operating expenses from income. There were three numbers to consider:

1. Income - did it increase or decrease over the year?
2. Was the expense item in keeping with the change in income?
3. Did the company bring in more or less cash than last year?

It is difficult to alter those numbers although some managements have been able to change sales and hence income by bringing future sales into the current reporting period or deferring them to a future date. Did the sale occur when the order was received, shipped or paid for? In the same way expenses can be shifted from period to period. I could go on ad nauseum as to how earnings can be "adjusted" but once again after having reached agreement on what are the corporation's real earnings, how much do you pay for them? Or in other words what P/E multiple do you attach to the earnings? To determine that multiple so as to be able to compare corporations as to their investment merit a number of basic questions have to be answered:

1. Does the company have a record of consistent earnings growth?

2. Are the earnings erratic?

3. Does the company give the shareholders a portion of the earnings as dividends?

4. Is that portion consistent?

Every prospectus for an investment product will always warn you that "Historical performance cannot assure future results". However what you do know is that if management remains in place the attitudes that gave you this year's earnings performance will be applied to next year.

After all this research you have decided that you would be willing to pay 15 times last year's earnings as a price for the shares. However to your surprise you find from the share price listings that similar companies to Mammoth (your target) are selling in a range of 10 times (cheap) to 20 times earnings (expensive). You are back to where you started in that you know the price of the company's shares but not their value. Is there any other measure to consider? Yes.

Yield: You could say let's put an end to all this theorizing and just get down to basics which is yield. The question is which yield, earnings or dividend? Obviously the earnings yield is just the earnings divided by the price of the shares (the P/E upside down) and not of much interest for this concept. What you really want to know is, how much is this company going to pay you per year to own a portion of it? You are obviously looking at the dividend and how much you would have pay for that.

There are a number of factors driving the price of a dividend paying share. The primary determinant is what the other income producing securities are paying, the other income paying securities being bonds. If high quality bonds with six months left to redemption are paying five percent it is unlikely that a company of the same quality would have a dividend yield at or approaching the bond yield. The reason being that there is a tax benefit to receive your payment as a dividend from the company rather than interest. The capital market participants will raise the price of the shares to such a level that the after tax yield to the investors is similar for both the bonds and shares of Mammoth Corporation. If the Mammoth's bonds are paying five percent you can expect that the dividend yield on its shares would be about 3.5 percent, not because of the value of the dividend but the price of the shares as dividend yield equals dividend amount divided by share price.

But once again as you view the yield on dividend paying shares at a time when Mammoth Corporation is yielding 3.5 percent you discover that there are others with yields as low as less than one percent to over eight percent. Obviously there is more than bond yields at work here. The yields are being affected by what speculators are assuming will be the performance of the share price. The less than one percent yield shares implies that that their price has been pushed up by expectations of some sort of corporate activity.

When looking at high yield shares it is not the expectation of corporate activity but consideration of the expectation of a continuing dividend stream at current levels. Speculators assuming that a dividend payment at current levels is unsustainable will sell the shares believing their price will retreat to a level where the new lower dividend provides a more appropriate yield. The lower price with the same dividend thus provides a higher yield.

Dividend evaluations are a little more concrete than trying to guess share prices. When looking at a corporation as a potential dividend payer the concepts that are important are how consistent is the dividend and what portion of earnings does it represent.

If the company has been paying the same proportion of its earnings as a dividend for an extended period then it is a worthy contender for your investment funds. Whatever you might be willing to pay for a company with a consistent dividend you would surely pay more for a company that continuously increases its dividend. What affects the dividend growth is a factor known as the payout ratio and earnings growth. If a company has a policy of paying 50 percent of its earnings out to the shareholders, then as the earnings increase so will the dividend. The obverse holds true in that if a company with a fixed payout ratio sees its earnings fall then it will cut its dividend.

A good example of companies with a payout ratio and increasing earnings are the Canadian banks. Dividend increases are only approved by the directors when they can feel secure that the current earnings increase is sustainable. An interesting aside of bank yields is that during the financial crisis of 2008 the yields on many Canadian bank shares for a time doubled, not because the banks increased their dividends but because panicky shareholders sold at any price their bank shares thus driving down prices.

The best answer: The best measure of how to value a share is look at the yield and work backwards. Having chosen a dividend paying stock next look at its P/E. If the P/E is higher than the company's peers then the market is expecting earnings growth. Will that growth be passed on to shareholders as the result of a defined payout ratio? A low P/E could be a reflection of doubts about the company's future earnings attainability.

Determine the book value per share (usually given in any reasonable research report) and divide the earnings per share and dividend by that amount. Does this reflect a reasonable return on investment? If not the assets are being underutilized and you should look elsewhere.

Sausages

We all know what sausages are, the internal skin of an animal stuffed with bits of meat. The investment market has an identical product and it was originally called the mutual fund in North America and the unit trust in Europe.

The way the investment market creates its "sausages" is by establishing a vessel or vehicle into which it can put the shares of different companies. This unit into which the shares have been deposited is then broken up into units and sold to the public. Let's start a mutual fund called the "Gargantuan Fund" with 100 units.

If we were to buy 100 shares of the Bank of Montreal for the fund then each unit would have the value of the same price as the Bank of Montreal. We, the fund managers, would set the price of the fund's units at the end of the trading day at the price of the Bank of Montreal and would be willing to buy or sell units to the public based on that price as one unit represents one share of the Bank of Montreal. We can neither gain nor lose by transacting the Gargantuan Fund shares at the price of the Bank of Montreal.

What happens if we now add 100 shares of the Bank of Nova Scotia to the fund? Then each fund unit would be the equivalent of the price of the two bank shares at the end of the trading day. There you have it. A mutual fund is a collection of shares thrown into a basket and sold off to the public. The mutual share originator has to be willing to buy or sell the units on the basis of the value of the underlying shares. Over time mutual funds have been formed to hold stocks of various industries and various countries. You can buy a fund with an oil, bank, mining or whatever industry you want representation in. You can buy a fund that imitates the New York Stock Exchange Index or the Standard and Poor's. Or you can buy a fund that is active in the market place buying and selling what the portfolio manager believes are the stars and the dogs of the future.

In this latter case, the successful fund managers are accorded star status. Peter Lynch ran the Magellan Fund for Fidelity investments which in most years managed to outperform the general market. He was regarded as a guru until he was no longer able to provide consistently better than market returns. Old time portfolio managers eventually begin to believe in the efficient market thesis and their portfolios start to resemble the index or market against which they are measured. These are the so called "closet indexers".

Mutual funds became a big business because the funds offered the unsophisticated investor the ability to have the services of some of the most agile, knowledgeable and clever investment professionals in the industry. For many years the mutual funds offered the small investor a simple way to participate in equity markets. However, some buyers failed to read the fine print disclaimer which usually said, "Past performance is no indicator of future performance". As well, when some of the more sophisticated mutual fund investors looked at the longer term performance of their investments they found that their mutual funds always seemed to slightly underperform in total return.

This resulted from two features of the fund, the first being that it always had to have cash on hand to repurchase units and was therefore never fully invested. The other drain on the mutual fund was the cost of running it. Someone had to pay the fund managers and it was the fund investor. These fees often ran as high as 2.5

percent per year up front. Then there was the back door. Some of the funds began paying advisors to keep clients in the firm's funds and these were known as trailer fees and were a drain on the fund.

Like so many good ideas the mutual fund became corrupted by greed. But as always the financial engineers found a solution, this being the Exchange Traded Fund or ETF. Mutual funds were inaugurated that matched various market segments from indices to commodities. These were listed on a stock exchange and the fund founders set an offering price at which they would issue the new units of the funds on the exchange. This was at a price equivalent to the intrinsic value of the units. The trading would be done by investors and it was unexpected that an ETF would seldom trade outside of its intrinsic value. The costs were negligible, hence the fees of less than 0.05 percent. At the time of this writing the ETF's had become the source of thirty percent of the share trading on any day on the exchanges. That is they bought and sold thirty percent of the trading volume on the exchanges. I am sure the question has already arisen in your mind. What happens if all the ETF fund managers have to sell or buy the same share on the same day to maintain the portfolio balance?

ETF's can be deemed the Black Plague of the investment industry. The retail, woman on the street, investor need only make one decision, "Do I want to be in the investment markets or not?" Once having set up her on line investment account she need only decide if she wants to own the gold, oil, real estate or broad market. Having done so, she purchases an ETF or sells her current position for a commission of $10.00.

As you can see this will mean the end of the mutual fund firms as we know them, the advisors and the wealth management firms. If your niece, Electra, is thinking of a career as an advisor or wealth manager I would suggest you steer her away from that.

The Investment Market's Credit Card

Yes, like shopping for a frock and accessories you can spend more in the investment market than what's in your purse. It is called credit at the shopkeepers and leverage at the brokers. You borrow from the vendor, whether broker or shopkeeper, to be able to buy more than you can afford. Borrowed from the shopkeeper it is credit, if borrowed from the broker it is called margin.

Your broker or whoever is holding your shares and bonds will allow you to borrow against those assets. Typically a broker will allow you to borrow 50 percent of the value of your shareholdings, 80 percent of the value of your corporate bond holdings and 90 percent of the value of your government bond position.

The result of that borrowing means that if you gave your broker $1,000 to invest in shares he can actually buy you $2,000 worth because you need only put up 50 percent of the cost. So with your $1,000 you could at the outset buy 20 shares of a $50.00 stock. The shares would be fully paid for and you owe your broker nothing. However because your shares are considered marginable you need only put up 50 percent of the value which means that you can buy an additional tranche of 20 shares (the new shares you are buying are also marginable) at $50.00 giving you a holding of 40 shares worth $50.00 each. Through borrowing against the shares you bought you can now double your position, however, remember that you owe the broker $1,000. You own 40 shares valued at $2,000 which forms the collateral against the $1,000 you owe your broker. The broker knows that you are more than willing to pay him interest on this borrowed money and your benefit is eroded by that cost.

If the shares were to slide in price to $40.00 each, your holding is now worth only $1,600 and you have to maintain a 50 percent asset position with your broker which is based on a value of $2,000. Your asset position is now only $800 (.5 X $1600) so the broker will ask you for another $200 ($200 + $800 = $1,000) to make your position fully covered. This is the dreaded "margin call".

The reason it is dreaded is because speculators who believe that their new found darling will soon sky rocket in price are willing to borrow to their limit from the casino, excuse me, broker, to increase their holding and hence potential profit. When the call comes for more cash to maintain the margin limits, many speculators are hard pressed to cover the increased amount required. On occasions, this causes selling to reduce the margin positioned and raise cash. This of course just puts more downward pressure on the share price exacerbating the need for more cash to cover the margin. It can cause a death spiral for speculative share prices.

Why would someone undertake such a risk, you may ask? In the example above if the shares had gone from the $50.00 purchase price to $80.00 you would have made $600 ($30 gain X 20 shares =$600) in an un-margined account because you only held 20 shares while you would have made $1,200 ($30 gain X 40 shares) if you had doubled your shareholding through margin.

For the real investor the concept of margin is as appetizing as eight day old fish. There is an occasion when you can turn this unwholesome device to your advantage. If you are in period of low interest rates where the broker is charging you an annualized rate of say three percent and your bank stock is paying 4.5 percent then why not double up? You are making an extra 1.5% which after tax is worth even more as the interest you pay is at fully deductible as a cost of doing business and the dividend is tax shielded to some extent.

I Feel Lucky

Well if you feel lucky today welcome to the Casino Exchange. We have lots of games for you to play and you don't even have to bother with buying any chips, excuse me I meant shares.

At some point in time it was deemed so inefficient and costly for the punters to have to buy actual shares to gamble on the stock exchange that someone invented options. An option is a contract. Someone, somewhere offers a contract to sell to you or buy from you a fixed number of shares at a fixed price for a fixed period. You will also hear these as referred to as "derivatives" as they are not an investment but derive from a security.

So let's assume that Mammoth Corporation shares are selling at $1,000 apiece. Your broker may be able to find someone willing to sell you a contract (a call) to deliver at your option 10 shares at $1,000 each for 6 months. To provide you that privilege the option provider wants you to pay her upfront $250. If during that period the share price of Mammoth never exceeds $1,000 you will not exercise your option and let it die at the end of 6 months and write off your $250 as a loss. However if Mammoth trades at $1,100 a share you would exercise you option to buy 10 share at $1,000, take delivery of the shares and sell them in the market place at $1,100. On your 10 shares you made a profit of $1,000 ($11,000 - $10,000 = $1,000) your cost to make that $1,000 was the price of the option which was $250 which leaves you a net profit of $750. You tripled your money!

More likely the transaction would have proceeded along the lines that you would sell the option you paid $250 for to a buyer at $1,000 which could be either the person who sold it to you or someone expecting a further rise in the share price. You could have made $750 on Mammoth shares without even having to have owned them. Similarly, if you believed that Mammoth shares were overpriced you could have bought a contract (a put) that would have given you the <u>option</u> to sell Mammoth shares at $900 apiece to the supplier of that contract for a fixed period. If the shares fall below that price you can either exercise your contract or sell it at its new higher price.

Amazing, you can profit on the change in Mammoth's share price without having to go through the inconvenience of actually owning them. Does that sound like investing to you? You could go to Woodbine Race Track, conclude that "Lucky Boy" was going to win the next race. Would you buy the horse or just go to the betting window and lay a bet?

Option trading is really a mugs game. To win your bet you must correctly guess the price direction of the share as well as the time window in which it is going to change. When asked about the direction of the gold price I always say it will double. I just don't say when and as such, at some point in time I will be correct. For a share speculator, which is akin to gambling, she need only get the direction correct, not when it will happen. For the option player, she must guess two issues correctly, what event will occur (price rise or fall) and the time in which it will happen. Lots of luck!

You may well ask why do otherwise moral people allow this sort of gambling to go on in what should be a serious undertaking such as investing. It came about in very early times, probably in ancient Greece. A farmer looking at his spring planting would want to insure that he obtained a reasonable profit. He would find a merchant willing to buy the crop upon harvest at a price fixed in advance. In modern parlance he would be seen as "hedging". Note that the merchant did not have the option of buying or not, he had to buy. The merchant as well had the right to sell that contract. If he felt that weather dictated that the crop would be poor that year he might sell his obligation to another speculator.

Those contracts were extended to include the option of buying the crop. Under those contracts the speculator paid the farmer for the right to buy the crop if he chose. He could, at exercise date, refuse to buy the crop and forego his option payment. The benefit to the farmer was that should the crop prove mediocre and the option not exercised he would have as revenue that year a reduced sales price for his crop but as well the option payment he received from the speculator.

As always the overseers of the market want to insure liquidity. In early times the barrel boys of London buying and selling shares for their accounts as brokers were assuming risks of owning the shares until a buyer could be found. They in effect had a crop that would be sold in the future. Maybe it was judicious to take out some crop insurance by hedging and so the options market was born.

In the same way by allowing the gamblers into the share market place the liquidity has been increased because now there is the capability of selling the shares to or buying from an option contract writer.

There is another form of market speculation which has a little more semblance of utility and that is short selling. Let's assume that you have heard that Mammoth Corporation directors have decided to colonize the oceans floors to accommodate the forthcoming overpopulation problem. In your mind this is going to be the greatest fiasco since farming on the moon. If you had any Mammoth stock you would sell it immediately but you don't own any. However, your hair dresser does. You ask him if he would lend you his shares for a couple of months. You both agree on a deposit and a fee to him for the loan. You now call your broker and tell him to sell 100 shares of Mammoth at $1,000. But you don't own any he retorts. You tell him you'll drop buy with the 100 shares on your way home from your hairdresser.

If the project gets tied up by governments and environmentalist leaving Mammoth bleeding money the shares collapse let's say to $500. You've just made $50,000 on Mammoth stock without ever having owned Mammoth shares. How did you make $50,000?

Sell 100 shares at $1,000   = $100,000
Buy 100 at shares at $500 to return to your hairdresser = $50,000
Net to you $50,000.

This kind of transaction had a legitimate place in share trading. Think of the barrel boy Nick who has just received an order from Lord Twitching his best customer for 100 shares of Hudson Bay. Nick doesn't have any shares of Hudson Bay but knows that Ralph has so he fills Lord Twitching's order and tells him to drop by tomorrow to pick up the shares. Nick borrows the shares from Ralph because he is short the stock. Nick then lets it be known amongst the clan of barrel boys that he is a buyer of Hudson Bay shares. There are two serious related dangers in short selling.

Assume that Lord Twitching was acting on inside information having learned in advance that the profits of the Hudson Bay Company were skyrocketing because the fashion of beaver pelt hats had now crossed the English Channel and sales were brisk. If the news came out before Nick managed to buy the shares he owed Ralph then he would now be trying to buy them at a much higher price than he sold them for assuming he can find a seller. He has to replace the shares at any cost or be barred from his trade. The problem Nick is facing is called a "short squeeze". This occurs when speculators buy shares knowing that a short position is developing but also aware that the short sellers have misinterpreted the market direction. A short squeeze is not uncommon as markets are efficient and random.

There is another problem that arises with a short squeeze; your potential loss is infinite if the shares go in the wrong direction. When you buy a share your potential loss is the amount you paid for it. It can go no lower than zero. When you have short sold a share there is no limit as to how high the price can go and hence your potential loss.

I mention the existence of these casino types of undertaking because I believe that at some time during your investing experience some neophyte in the business will tell you of the satyr who made a fortune trading options and retired to open a unicorn ranch. As you know both the satyr and the unicorn are mythical as is the fortune that was generated.

Weird Science

It was a dark and stormy early night in 1900's Springfield, Massachusetts, while John Magee worked feverishly on his new scheme in his windowless office. It had windows but these were boarded over so that he wouldn't be bothered by any outside influences and no one could see what would be his creation. With his green eye shade and spring clip shirt sleeve bands no one could tell if he was on the verge of a scientific breakthrough or nervous breakdown. Soon his dream of turning pencil lead into gold would be revealed and investors would be hauling him down Wall Street in a sedan chair proceeded by nubile maidens throwing rose petals before him. John Magee had invented stock charting as a method of forecasting share prices. By plotting the volume, share price fluctuation and closing price of a share over time on a piece of grid paper, John Magee could show that if a share price was going upwards on his chart it would continue to do so – until it stopped. Also, if a share price graph line was going down this would continue until such time as it stopped. What could be simpler? And worthless? The fact that a chart of share prices could no sooner predict that a company would invent the semi-conductor, the polio vaccine or the instant camera was immaterial to the voodoo crowd. The astrological crowd, fortune tellers and otherwise sane people leapt on this new stock market device with its science devoted to 'head and shoulders' formations, pennants, wedges moving averages and breakdowns. It was like magic. When a stock collapsed, within days a chart would be published showing this had happened. The chart was implacable – and historical, or should I say hysterical.

When share trading results are posted to a chart they reflect trends already occurring. A chart pattern of a stock going down will not show a return to positive territory until after the event has occurred by which time it is too late to buy. Similarly when a share price turns negative the stock plotter doesn't know about it until after it has occurred and he plots it on his chart.

I remember just before the Bre-X share collapse that our firm's chartist told me the pattern showed a 'flag' that was indicating serious upside potential for the share price. It was in the jargon, going to breakout. Days later when the scandal was revealed and the share price collapsed, I asked him about his chart. He said it was all there in the chart before the announcement, in that what he thought was a 'flag' was actually a 'wedge' which tuned into a 'head and shoulders', a sure sign of impending share price collapse. When I mentioned that the head and shoulders could only be discerned after the fact, he abruptly left the water cooler and said that he was returning to his computer graphics program to pray for my redemption. I noticed subsequently that in his office he had a number of dolls with likenesses of some of our firm's members. There were pins sticking out of some of them.

If it were that simple your broker would arrive in his office in the morning and demand all the charts of upward bound share prices and buy those. He would then view the charts of the downward moving shares and short sell those before heading for lunch at the yacht club aboard his new $2 million Hinckley sloop. Needless to say John Magee did not die a rich man. Hindsight is always 20/20.

What stops the chartist in their tracks is the efficient market theory and the randomness of share prices. The first person to enunciate the randomness of share price movements was the famous financier John Pierpont Morgan. As he stepped out of his office on a morning in 1907 after having formed a syndicate to save the US economy and currency a reporter asked him what the stock market would do now. His answer, "It will fluctuate".

The efficient market thesis states that all the past, present and future information regarding a company is currently reflected in its share price. This was best described by Burton Malkiel in his book "A Random Walk Down Wall Street" first published in 1973 and still selling well after every market meltdown. He proves time and again that a passive portfolio invested in a broad range of stocks will outperform an actively managed one by leaps and bounds. In most years seventy five percent of the professional money managers will underperform the index against which they are measured. The reason your mutual fund does not do better than the market, although managed by a rocket scientist, is that the fund has to have a certain amount in cash to accommodate redemptions, there are fees as high as 2.5% of your investment taken annually and the size problem[13]. Your mutual fund manager cannot dedicate research time to start-ups such as Microsoft was at its outset. The amount of stock your fund manager could buy in a start-up is limited by the supply available. Instead he has to turn his attention to the industry giants where there is market liquidity[14] and an abundance of research. This means big companies like General Motors, Citibank and AIG. And so the random walk begins with baby footsteps and the market

---

13 If a company has a million shares outstanding and the price of a single share is $5.00 the market capitalization is said to be 5 million dollars ($5.00 X 1 million shares). If a portfolio manager needs a million dollar exposure to a company to be meaningful in his portfolio then in this case he would have to own 200,000 shares or 20 percent of the company. This would not be considered good portfolio practice.

14 Liquidity refers to the amount of stock being traded daily or weekly and the ability to fit one's activity within that trading. If a stock is described as "thin" it means that there is little daily volume of trading and hence acquiring or selling a position difficult.

professionals help maintain the stride, keeping the market efficient by acting on all the historic and perceived future information.

You may well ask, "How did Warren Buffet manage to do so well"? Because his broker didn't. What broker wants a client who would buy Coca Cola shares and hold them for 22 years? You don't get to be commodore of the yacht club with clients like that. Buffet bought the shares of well managed companies with a dominant position in a growing market. If any of those basic factors changed he would sell his position. In response to a question regarding his success he answered he never bought shares he bought companies. **To him it was immaterial what the daily price of Coca Cola shares was. His interest was the company - not its share price.**

So, dear lady, how does this equate to your universe? Let's say you are shopping for a new dishwasher. When you arrive at the appliance dealers he tells you this G.E. model is selling very well and is bargain priced. If you were a chartist you would say that the volume of trade is on the upside and the price firming. Looks like the G.E. is the one. But then you notice the other machines off to the side out of prominent view. There are Mieles, Bosch and Kitchen Aid just to mention a few. You decide that rather than be a chartist you will do some fundamental analysis, so you buy a copy of 'Consumer's Guide' as you leave the appliance dealers. That night after having to do the dishes by hand seeing as the beast in the kitchen won't work (I refer to your dishwasher – not your spouse) you sit down with a glass of sherry and read what your 'Consumer's Guide' has to say about dishwashers. You find that of all the models tested the G.E., was not the highest rated. In fact the new G.E. model with all the fancy features hasn't been released to the market and not yet available for testing by the magazine's researchers. So that explains the low price and high volume. The dealers are blowing off the old models in anticipation of the new release. What about the others? It seems the Bosch is very highly rated so the next morning you return to the smiling man in the dishwasher section of the appliance section.

You ask about the Bosch. His response is that it is a nice machine but expensive, look at the money you are going to save on the G.E. as opposed to the higher priced machines. Seeing as you don't want to come back to buy another machine from him within the next decade you choose the machine which fundamental research says should meet your requirements for years to come although the chart on the G.E. looks fabulous. Yes, you could have bought two G.E.'s for the price of one Bosch but then who wants a couple of louts under the sink cursing as they try to remove your old dishwasher every five years to put in a new one? Not to mention having to enrich the appliance salesman every five years rather than ten.

So with the security purchase it's better to buy something that has intrinsic value rather than a share based on a chart of what has happened in the recent past as the future is random and the chart is history.

You probably are curious as to why chart based investors exist. Like the searchers for the fountain of youth wandering around Central America they know that there is something better than just buying and holding a share. These people refuse to believe that there are people as clever as they are who have considered all that is known about a company and its shares and have come to a collective agreement on its value.

Consider this, if share charts correctly forecast the future price direction of shares even 55 percent of the time there would be a rush to share charting as an investment strategy and the advantage soon lost. Conversely, if this didn't happen the world would be awash in unicorn ranches.

Of Corporate Bondage

When companies sell shares from their treasury the existing share-holders have the value of their holding diminished. If the net assets of Mammoth Corporation are worth $100 and there are 100 shares outstanding, each share represents $1.00 in value ($100 of assets/100 shares). If the company issues another 100 shares so that there are in total 200 shares outstanding the intrinsic value of each share has fallen to $0.50 ($100 of assets/200 shares ignoring whatever funds where raised). You may well ask why would Mammoth Corporation issue a further 100 shares? Let us assume that the company has just finished developing a great new software package but has no money to market the product. By raising more money from the public the marketing program can be pursued and the product sold. Again the question arises; why not just borrow the money from a bank? The problem with banks is not, can you borrow, but whether they will lend.

A bank would be willing to lend to Mammoth if the company had a tried and proven product generating a continuous flow of income. The reason being that if the bank did not receive either its interest or principal it could seize the product, sell it, and recoup its loan or a portion of it. In this case, we have an untried product and no income. There is another alternative and that is to borrow from the investing public. However, the public is as discerning as the bank manager and there can be no loan forthcoming for Mammoth Corporation from the public, hence the share offering.

But let's proceed a few years to the point where Mammoth is coining money with their new software through monthly licensing fees. The managers of the company realize that there is the potential for an add on product that would double income. Sixty million would be required to develop and market this but the company only has $10 million in its bank account.

The bank manager can't see his way clear to loan money to Mammoth as their assets, although valuable, are not immediately saleable. The banker is looking at what would happen if Mammoth missed a payment of interest or the principal at the end of the loan. The banker would foreclose on the company and seize its assets. It would now be the owner operator of a software company. Banks lend and borrow money (a deposit in a bank is a loan by the depositor to the bank). They do not want to own houses from foreclosed mortgages or businesses from failed loans. When the bank forecloses on a defaulted loan it would prefer to have some asset backing the loan that can be easily monetized. Up until recently, residential real estate had that capability. At a price you could find a buyer. If the house had been mortgaged to 75% of its appraised value the bank, at foreclosure, could discount the house sale price by up to 25% before it had to take a loss.

Rather than dilute the holding of Mammoth's existing share-holders further let's consider another loan alternative, the public. Obviously it is going to be difficult although not impossible to find one lender to advance the money to the company. The long shot one lender possibilities are pension funds and merchant banks. A pension fund upon default has the deep pockets necessary to hold the assets until a suitable buyer can be found. A merchant bank would have determined an exit strategy prior to making the loan. However these avenues are difficult to navigate and an easier approach is to find an investment firm willing to syndicate the loan.

If Mammoth wanted to borrow $50 million the investment firm would break the loan into 50,000 bonds of $1,000 each and sell those to the public. Now the difficult part begins. What interest rate is Mammoth willing to pay and what is the least the investor will accept? When the new issue bond is offered to you the question that will bedevil you is are you receiving interest commensurate with the risk you are undertaking? The risks are that Mammoth will default on either its interest or principal payment to you.

At this point it is worth looking at the mechanics of this financing. What the investment firm is going to do is underwrite the loan issue. That means it will put up the money required and then sell paper to the public witnessing the public's participation in the loan. The piece of paper issued to the investor is the borrowing company's pledge that it will pay the bearer of that piece of paper interest at a certain rate on the principal amount ($1,000) per bond on certain dates, and at another date in the future it will redeem the bond by paying back the principal to the certificate holder. In other words this is a typical loan agreement like you might have with one of your children. For example your son approaches you and says he wants to buy a new car and needs $20,000. You make a deal, he pays you $600 interest every New Year's Day and the $20,000 on New Year's Day three years hence. You might even draw up a simple contract to bind the agreement.

With the corporate loan the mechanics are a little more complicated. The investment firm, once it has sold the loan, considers itself out of the picture. So the question arises as to who is going to send you your interest cheques and the principal when due; a trustee will. This organization will be hired by the investment firm to handle all the financial details of the obligation. To receive the funds the borrower has to contract with the trustee to pay the interest and principal on time. Assets may or may not be pledged against the loan. The company, if it is of the utmost credit worthiness, may pledge the "company's full credit". In other words should the payments not be made the company becomes the property of bond holders.

The borrower might limit their liability by pledging a particular asset such as a building or factory. For our example let's say we have created a bond with the backing of the full credit of the company to pay back the loan in 5 years' time and in the interim pay each $1,000 bondholder $25 interest on June 30th and December 30th a total of $50 for the year. The Great Imperial Trust Company is the trustee and has provided Mammoth with the funds (raised by selling the bonds/debentures through an investment dealer) in exchange for a signed undertaking (indenture) to meet the payment obligations. Now we have created a bond/debenture with a affixed coupon rate ($25 + $25 = $50/$1000 = 5%) and a redemption date. Now comes the tough part.

Yield to Maturity — Is that the Time After Adolescence?

When you serve up a fine tasting meal there are those at the table that in spite of their girth will ask for another portion. With a bond offering the situation is the same. If the issue is perceived as a solid or low credit risk and the interest rate high then the buyers will ask for more than is available. The issue will be described as oversubscribed. In our case, if Mammoth Industries is oversubscribed with its $50 million, five year, 5% bond then the buyers and the sellers are more than happy. The company however is not. They perceive that they have given away too much in the market place. Perhaps there would not have been such a rush to buy if the interest rate had been 4.75% or 4.50%. The investment firm that brought the issue to market (underwriter) will receive irate calls from its client, Mammoth Industries, complaining that the rate was set too high to aid the sales campaign. To add salt to the wound the company will note to the underwriter that the deal was so good for investors that the bond is now trading in the market at $1,100 a premium to its issue price of $1,000.

Therein lays a major problem. It's like putting a sauce on a meal. There is a fine line between too little (the age of the fish shows through) or too much and you can't taste the fish at all. In the ways that cooks adjust sauces, the underwriters of bonds adjust interest rates and issue prices[15]. If the rate is set too high then the ultimate penalty for the borrower is bankruptcy from unsustainable interest charges. Set the rate too low and the borrower's issue won't be sold and the company will die from the lack of capital. Goldilocks porridge dilemma all over again – not too hot, not too cold.

But it gets better. What if I were to phone you and say that on August 31, 3 years from today you will be able to sell for $1,000 an investment you can buy from me today for $910. If I did that the regulators would commit violent acts to my body such as crucifixion. The reason is that no one can predict the price of a share in three years' time. But I can predict the price of a bond on its redemption day. The price will be $1,000. If as and when the loan represented by the bond gets refunded the bond holders get $1,000 for their paper irrespective of what they paid for it. So let's follow the course of life for the 5% Mammoth Industries bond.

The bond was issued two years ago at par ($1,000). That is each purchaser had to put up $1,000 to own one bond. Every August 31 and February 28th the bond holders receive $25 per bond representing two interest payments per year for a total of $50 per year or an annual return of 5% ($50/$1000). However today with the sales of its anti-depressant drug slowing and earnings crumbling there are doubts in the financial markets that Mammoth will be able to pay back the original $50 million borrowed. Having been aware of the company's problems you do some research and determine that there is the possibility of their anti-depressant drug being approved in the UK which with its abysmal, depressing climate makes an

---

15   If the issue appears difficult to sell at par because of what appears to be a mean interest rate, the underwriter may sell the issue at slight discount to par thus enhancing the purchaser's return.

anti-depressant a certain best seller. You call your friendly broker and ask him if there is a quote or market for the bond. He confirms that the bond is on offer for sale at $910 and being bid to purchase at $860. Actually the numbers he will quote you are $86 and $91 which in reality means 10 times that price. Being fairly confident that the bond will be redeemed at the end of its life you calculate what you will make if you buy one of these bonds as offered at $910 today three years before redemption.

The best way to look at the situation is that in three years' time you will get $1,000. So that would imply that you are getting $30 per year as part of the discount:

Redemption price:	$1,000
Purchase price:	$910
Difference:	$90

The amount of the difference in what you paid for the bond $910 and what you will get is $90 ($1000 – $910) and you can look at averaging it out to $30 per year ($90/3 = $30)

This is called recouping the discount as you approach maturity. The amount you earn annually is thus $30 of principal and $50 of interest for a total of $80 per year. You investment return or **yield to maturity** is:

Interest and principal earned	=	$80 ($50 + $30)
Amount invested	=	$910
Return = earnings/investment	=	$80/$910 = 8.79%

It would almost appear as a slight of hand that we have changed a 5% bond into a bond yielding 8.79%. No, it was all above board. Even if we had disregarded the recovery of the discount of $90 from the redemption price and only looked at the simple yield that is cash interest divided by cash purchase price our yield (the **"simple" yield** in the vernacular) would be:

Interest earned	$50
Cost of investment	$910
Return = interest/investment =	$50/$910 = 5.49%

The individual purchasing the bond at the issue price of $1,000 will always have a yield of 5%. However the person who pays a different price will have a different yield because **although the price has changed the amount of interest paid annually stays the same.**

I am sure that you have concluded that if a bond can sell at a discount in the aftermarket it could just as well sell for a premium. You must keep in mind that when a bond is issued, the coupon or dollar amount of interest paid annually is fixed irrespective of interest rate market conditions or perception of the bonds quality. You as the holder of a 5 percent bond will always receive $50 per year irrespective of what you paid for it. Your simple interest rate is the amount of dollar interest divided by the bond purchase price. What could cause a bond to sell for a premium?

Let's say that you were astute enough to have purchased a Bell Canada 5 percent bond at par when issued 9 years ago. It was issued for a period of ten years which means that it has only 1 year to go to refunding or redemption. Over the next year you will receive $50 for the year as interest. You are concerned that when this bond is redeemed the only similar quality offered bonds in the new issue market or aftermarket are offering 2 percent or $20 a year. Would you sell your bond at par to yield 5 percent when others are selling theirs to yield only 2 percent? Most certainly not.

For the investor who is buying your old bond to net a 2 percent yield she must lose some amount of money from the $50 interest payment to bring her income down to equal the $20 she would receive from a new bond. That means over the next year she can afford to lose $30 on the bond and would still end up with the equivalent of 2 percent. Let's look at the calculation.

Income calculation:

Interest earned	= $50.00
	Minus $30.00 excess purchase payment
Total Return	$20.00

Interest rate calculation:

Income earned/invested funds
$20/ $1030 = 1.94%

If the payment to purchase the bond is decreased to $1029.60 from $1030.00 the new owner of the bond will earn exactly 2 percent while receiving a coupon payment of $50.00. Why would she pay you $1,029.60 for a bond that will only give her $1,000 in a year's time? Because she cannot find in the market place or in the new issues being offered any equivalent quality bond that will yield her more than 2 percent for one year. She either pays you $1,029 and receives $50.00 for the year or she pays $1,000 to the new issue broker for a bond that will pay her $20.00 for the year. **Either way she will earn her 2 percent per year.**

Many investors are confused when they hear that yields are rising because the bond market is falling. That has to be true because the amount of interest being paid is the same, however, the price (the divisor in the equation) is decreasing thus giving a larger final answer. Investors are thus having to put up less money today to purchase a bond to get the same dollar amount of interest, hence yield must be higher.

What you should take away from this is:

- Coupon is the interest rate set for the bond or debenture in perpetuity
- Simple yield is the coupon divided by whatever you paid for the bond
- Yield to maturity is the effective interest rate you will earn after allowing for the return of discount from $1,000 (par) or the payment of premium you paid over par.

The Most Powerful Force on Earth

Bill Clinton's campaign manager, Jim Carville, once famously remarked that he wanted to be reincarnated as the bond market because, "You can intimidate everybody". Thus it was the most powerful force on earth.

What Carville was referring to is the fact that everybody borrows money, governments, companies and individuals. The level of interest rates will determine the ease at which they can obtain funds and the pain inflicted by those rates. As you saw previously yields are determined by the fixed coupon or interest rate and the floating price of a bond. In that example bonds of three year duration and similar quality are yielding 5.49 percent. Who in his right mind would lend three year money for any less than 5.49 percent or expect to get a return for three years of any more than 5.49 percent? In that way the bond market will dictate the interest paid by government, corporations and will influence how much you can borrow and hence spend. Therefore, interest rates will influence governments if they want to undertake an optional war and corporations if they are considering expansion. This powerful instrument would sound like something you should consider for your portfolio.

A bond or debenture is a note given to an investor indicating indebtedness. Usually the term bond is reserved for a government IOU and debenture for corporate notes, but in recent years the terms have become interchangeable. The note or security provided to the lender states that the borrower will pay the holder of the note a fixed sum at set dates[16] and then return his capital (principal) of $1,000 at some date in the future. This differs from a mortgage in that there is no payment of principal amount included in the periodic payments to the lender. Unlike its near cousin, the dividend, there is no flexibility in the amount of the interest payment, while a dividend's payment size is determined by the board of directors of the corporation. There is another difference between a bond and a dividend in that interest accrues every day and when you buy a bond you must pay the vendor the amount of interest already earned and yet to be paid.

For example if you were thinking of buying a 5 percent bond a day before one of its semi-annual interest payments you would have to pay the vendor for the interest she earned for 181 days as the interest periods are divided into two 182 tranches to make up the annual payment. The vendor would have received half her annual interest payment or $25.00 had she held the bond for 182 days but instead must settle for an abbreviated payment or:

Semi-annual payment for 182 days	=	$25.00
Amount earned per day = $25.00/182	=	$0.1374
Prorated payment for 181 days of interest = $0.1374 X 181days	=	$24.86

---

16 In North America bonds and debentures pay interest semi-annually whereas in the UK they mostly pay annually. In Europe there are both annual and semi-annual payment schedules.

If you had agreed to pay the vendor par for her bond you would as well have to pay her $24.86 in earned interest for a total of $1,024.86. Of course a day later when the interest is paid you will receive from the trustees $25.00 in interest.

Dividends do not accrue, meaning accumulate[17]. No one can be sure if the dividend for the next quarter will be paid or not. If you were to buy a share the day before the dividend is declared and are holding it when payable, you get the entire dividend. If on the other hand you sell a share the day before the dividend is declared payable you are entitled to none of the payout. With a bond, if you sell it the day before payout of the interest, the buyer pays you the interest and she starts to accrue interest from that date. Bonds are not well discussed in the business press as they are said to be too difficult to understand, there is little retail trade in bonds and some confusion.

Let's be truthful[18], bonds are not difficult to understand. Suppose your nephew came to you and asked to borrow $10,000 to finance his new bicycle courier business for five years. After determining when he will repay the loan and what interest rate will be set on the loan, you then ask him to explain his business plan and how it will enable him to pay the interest he has promised (hence a promissory note) and the principal on due date. If his projections are realistic you lend him the money and he gives you an IOU binding him to pay both interest and principal. He is therefore bound by his bond. What immediately comes to mind is that the piece of paper he gives you attesting to his indebtedness and obligation to pay you interest at set dates is, in the terms of the investment industry, illiquid. Your funds are trapped in this investment until repayment date as there is no "secondary market" for this paper. You participated

---

17   Preferred shares have been issued that have the feature that unpaid dividends accumulate to be paid in the future. These are referred to as "cumulative preferreds"

18   Some of the bias against bonds in the retail brokerage trade may stem from the fact that they are a no or low profit entity for the retail broker.

in the original issue of the paper but after that sale to you there is nowhere that you can sell it. However, in the broader corporate markets, things are different.

There is a vibrant market in corporate bonds. On any given day double the value of bonds will be traded on the world's exchanges compared to shares. Some of them are listed on exchanges while others trade over the counter, meaning that an informal market exists where buyers and sellers can get together for a transaction. The bonds listed for trading on exchanges are most often corporate convertible debentures. These are a hybrid between a share and a debenture and I will discuss them further in the text.

The most common form of debenture or bond is the "straight" which has no other features than its term (how long it will be around) and its interest rate (what it is going to pay you). The largest single issuer of this kind of paper is government. In more honest times governments only borrowed money to finance capital projects such as roads, bridges and dams. Their paper was thus considered to be of the highest quality because it was backed by assets and had the full taxing power of the government to pay its interest and principal when due. Then came wars. A war is an existential threat to government and as a result it is necessary for the government to take any means to preserve its existence including borrowing copious amounts to finance the conflict. At the end of the hostilities there are no new productive assets to provide income such as a new road, bridge or dam might do and so taxation must come to bear on the problem.

One of the experiences for governments has been that the populace does not take well to taxation for the purposes of war. To begin with there is conscription where the government has taxed the citizenry by taking away their sons and seldom returning them in the same condition it obtained them. There is little recourse to that form of taxation. The method of avoidance of increased monetary taxation was found through the implementation of currency inflation.

By devaluing the purchasing power of the national currency the purchasing power of the debt incurred is diminished hence in real terms the amount paid back to the lenders is reduced. Therefore wars often lead to inflation. That includes wars on drugs, poverty, terrorism, fascism and any other kind of "ism" you may consider. There is protection against inflation devaluing the real worth of your investment which I will discuss.

Then there is the confusion. The press and your local broker will on occasion refer to the "bond market" and what they are referring to is the market in government securities, not all debt securities which includes corporate and convertibles. You used to hear the statement, "stocks always outperform bonds" which turned out to be false in the first decade of the twentieth century so the statement was changed to, "stocks outperform bonds in the long run". That statement does not discern between the different types of bonds and what constitutes the long run. If you look at the period 1924 to 1964 the United States universe of "BBB" bonds provided a real return of 5.75% far surpassing the US stock market during that period[19]. You will note that the period included the great depression during which the default rate was 4% for corporate bonds. That meant 4% of the companies went into default but that does not mean the bond holders lost all their capital. **In corporate bankruptcies the bond holder gets paid the remainder of the corporate assets usually leaving the shareholders with nothing.**

If the speaker claims that shares out perform government bonds over the long term she is mostly correct, the reason being that the yield on government bonds in recent decades has been about 4 to 5%. Bearing in mind that inflation has stood at about 2% the real yield has been 2 to 3%. The US stock market has had a real return over the long haul (100 years)[20] of about 6% most of which was

---

19   If you had bought US Steel in 1928 you would not have seen that purchase price again until 1956 and even then it was in inflated not real dollars

20   Over the period 1950 to 2010 the return was 7.0 percent

dividends. The reason that governments can pay such paltry rates of interest is that there has existed over periods of time the belief that government bonds were the safest of all investments. There is an inherent flaw in that statement in that a French philosopher once stated, "Democracy will always collapse as the citizens will always vote for themselves more than what they can pay for". Greece is a classic example of that eventuality. Every politician running for election has to promise even more services and goods than her competitor and what previously was delivered. To pay for her promises she must either raise taxes or borrow money. Raising taxes is visible and painful to the electorate. Borrowing money is not. Eventually all that borrowing comes due for payment and you have the resulting default or near default of government. If the government defaults there are no assets to seize, unlike a corporate failure, and you could be left with nothing. Government defaults typically offer the debt holders new paper which has a portion of the face value of the original, in a devalued currency with little liquidity. The prestige of government paper based on the ability to tax is as false as the taut face you see on the 70 year old presenting the TV news telling of the great new benefit being bestowed through the munificence of government.

Passing Notes

Remember when you were in high school how your friends would pass you a piece of paper during class. Some of those notes would contain promises. The investment market has exactly the same device. The origin of the financial markets notes is somewhat different from the high school scenario but does entail a promise.

Financial notes or discounted bills go back to Renaissance times when the introduction of Arabic numbers made the calculation of interest feasible. However, the religious orders, whether eastern or western, opposed the payment of interest as all interest was considered usury. It could be logically claimed that if one sold a discounted bill and redeemed it at par that no interest was paid and the sin of usury not committed. How do these work?

There are two ways your nephew can borrow money from you for a year. He can borrow $100 and offer to pay you $110 in a year's time (at maturity) or you could offer him $91.91 today for which he would pay you $100 at maturity. In the first instance he is paying you your principal and interest. In the second you are earning money for providing capital but the interest feature is built into the security without being described as such. Either way, you earn 10 percent on your money. If your nephew accepts the latter choice he will give you a promissory note to pay you $100 in a year's time in exchange for $91.91.

Let's say your brother knows of his son's indebtedness and wants to clean up the family finances. He informs you he is aware that his son borrowed $91.91 from you six months ago and has promised to pay you $100 in another six months' time. Your brother would like to buy the note from you and is willing to give you the $91.91 his son borrowed in exchange for the note.

Not so fast, you say. That note was worth $91.91 six months ago as it had a year to lapse before redemption at $100. It is now more valuable as there are only six months left to redemption or maturity. You demand $95.35 which your brother realizes is a fair price. Also, there is no obligation for your brother to hold the note. He could sell it to some other family member while taking into account the change in value as redemption/maturity nears.

The approach of redemption is not the only factor affecting the price of a note. There is as well the interest rate environment. If at the time you lent to your nephew interest rates for private loans were in the ten percent range any of the family members would be willing to buy the note from you on the basis of its yielding ten percent to maturity. But what if during the loan period interest rates shot up to twenty percent? What would an investor pay for a note maturing in 6 months if the current notes are being issued with a 20 percent interest rate? By purchasing a six month note at $91.29 the investor would earn over that period the equivalent of 20 percent on his money.

There are two important concepts here. A discounted note (you are buying a loan worth $100 at a discount) will be priced on the basis of the current interest rate environment and the time to maturity. Those are the same two determinants in the price of a bond. Remember that a bond is a note issued at par, redeemable at par and paying a fixed annual dollar amount of interest which is expressed as its interest rate. The table below shows the effect of pricing of notes at various time and interest rates.

$100 PRINCIPAL DISCOUNTED
AT 1, 5 AND 10% OVER 1, 5 AND 10 YEARS.

YEARS	RATE	PRICE
1	1%	99.01
5	1%	95.15
10	1%	90.53
1	5%	95.24
5	5%	78.35
10	5%	61.39
1	10%	91.91
5	10%	66.26
10	10%	45.31

There is an interesting feature of that table if you look at one year and ten year discount for the various interest rates. The longer the period of time the deeper the discount, which fits with our intuitive conclusion. Apply that thinking to the bond market and what you will conclude is that if current interest rates go from one percent to ten percent in the marketplace the bonds which will suffer the greatest price contraction are the long dated ones.

Notes are commonly used by corporations to "park" money while waiting for an event such as a payment under a contract with a note being purchased to mature at the time the payment comes due. Commonly the effective interest rate you will earn on a note is better than what you will receive from a bank savings account. Discounted notes are issued by any variety of lenders from corporations to banks. The ones most suitable to the investing public are from the banks.

In periods of high interest rates it is not uncommon for pensioners to place their investments in bank notes on what is called a "ladder". Here the investor might purchase equal amounts of 6 month, one year and 2 year notes, or any combination of time periods and proportions of her capital. As the notes came due the investor would pocket an amount for current expenses and re-invest the balance in another series of notes.

The appeal of notes as an investment tool is their precision. You know what you are going to get and when you are going to get it. That combined with low transaction costs make them a stronger competitor for investor dollars in high interest environments.

The Takeover Hangover

There is a perception amongst some investors that the payment of a dividend is as welcome as a visit of one of the four horsemen of the apocalypse. They will tell you that the company paying a dividend has ended its period of expansion and it won't be long until another Nortel or Kodak moment, namely corporate death. This is the attitude prevalent in the growth cult which believes that the board and management of a corporation should invest all the shareholders money until it is all gone. The fallacy, of course, is that the corporate executives (directors and managers) were hired to run a company, not invest the shareholder's funds. They are especially incompetent at investing or they would be working in the investment industry. When I was a young mining analyst the famous International Nickel Company of Canada (INCO) announced one day that the board had agreed to management's purchase of a battery company for a quarter of a billion dollars. I went on to the sales floor of my employers and asked a grizzled veteran of the battle for investment survival what he thought of such an undertaking. His response was, "What do a bunch of mining engineers who have spent the last 25 years in a 3,000 foot hole in the ground know of investing?" He was of course right in that the investment destroyed two decades of dividend payouts and then led to the eventual disappearance of the company.

When a company announces the takeover of another firm what you will often see is a fall in the share price of the acquirer and a rise in the price of the acquired. There is enough common sense in the market place to know that an acquisition is risky at the best of times and likely not in the best interest of the acquiring shareholders[21]. Some managers have made a reasoned argument that a company should integrate vertically. That is how the car companies evolved. General Motors bought up its suppliers such as the electrical parts supplier Delco-Remy for good business reasons. The company became more integrated and had better control over its production chain. General Motors did not believe that it had to integrate horizontally by buying oil companies. There are acquisitions that are made from a business point of view to maximize profits. But how can you justify a gold mining company buying another mining entity, oil company or real estate venture? It has all been done with the attendant destruction of shareholder wealth. If you were the owner of the shares of Solid Gold Bar Mines I think you would prefer to make the choice of whether to invest in the shares of Dry Gulch Mines yourself with your dividends rather than have the directors of your firm make that decision for you. Such arrogance! They believe that their shareholders can't see a good investment when it is staring them in the face. I have always maintained that if the shareholders are too unsophisticated as to be able to invest their earnings from your company, Mr. Manager, then they must be a pretty stupid bunch to have invested in your company as well.

The question that the growth investors and traders will ask you, if you insist on being paid for the use of your money is, "Where will the corporations obtain the funds to grow?" Firstly the question arises as to what need is there to grow other than organically

---

21   As for the vending or selling shareholders, their shares would have been perfectly priced as a result of the "Efficient Market Thesis" prior to the takeover announcement and therefore require a premium to cause them to part with their shares. The purchasers are paying more than the market perceives as fair value.

through bigger market share, better products and excellent service? If the management can't accomplish that they should be fired. As to growth outside of the current product line or service, that can be arranged in the same way that the company started in the first instance and that is the investment markets. Who better to decide as to the worthiness of a new venture than potential new shareholders or bondholders? If Inco had gone to its bankers or share underwriters and said, we want to raise a quarter of a billion dollars to buy a battery company, once the laughter ceased, they would have been politely refused and the company might still exist.

A more recent example of corporate hubris can be seen in the recent history of Barrick Gold. American Barrick was purchased from Gary Last by Peter Munk and renamed Barrick Gold Corporation. Munk went about acquiring irrelevant minor gold mines and companies and at one point acquired through that process a very competent mine operator and geologist as part of a company purchased. They in turn brought into production for Barrick a highly profitable mine in Nevada. In the past decade that company has thrown off about a billion dollars a year in cash flow. Little of that went to the shareholders. Instead that accumulated ten billion dollars plus another $14 billion was invested on behalf of the shareholders in projects that were written off as worthless. If you add the $10 billion to the $14 billion that is a total of $24 billion invested on behalf of the shareholders and then determined to be worthless. That equates to $24 per share over the ten year period. The share price at this writing was around $20 per share. It is no accident that the major investors in the company want to see some changes on the board.

There is more damning evidence of the takeover game. I believe in the efficient market thesis which states that all the evidence available will lead to a security being priced to perfection in the market. In other words the stock market is telling you that as of this moment and these market conditions the share price you see quoted is exactly what the share is worth. The market works. If you don't believe this then you would be a fool to go anywhere near a stock market. Logically if the shares of "Takeover Target Corp" are trading at $10.00 that is what they are worth. For "Acquirer Corp" to take over "Takeover Target Corp" it will have to pay a premium over what the shares are really worth. If that is the case then what you should see is on the day of the announcement by "Acquirer Corp" that it is pursuing an acquisition in the market place its share price will fall and the target company's will rise. Why? Because the market realizes that "Acquirer Corp" is paying a premium for its purchase thus diluting the value of its existing shares.

If you are clever enough to invest in Mammoth Industries you're clever enough to invest the earnings generated by that company. For the company to undertake the investment function for you is an act of gross disdain for your intelligence on the part of management.

Have I Got An Investment For Us. It is Us!

A not too recent investment discovery by a number of managers and boards has been their own shares. Companies in recent years feeling unable to part with the accumulated shareholder earnings (at the time of this writing $565 billion in Canada) have decided to buy back some of their shares and have them cancelled. This is probably the least harmful investment management can make as they well know the company whose shares they are buying and therefore there can be no undisclosed liabilities or risks in buying its shares.

When I was a financial analyst I noticed a company that had reported losses in each of the past 5 years and increased book value per share in each of those years. That would seem counterintuitive. How can a company lose money every year and have the real value of its shares increase? What happened was that the company was indeed reporting operating losses but was cash income positive. The losses were caused by heavy non-cash financial charges.

For reporting purposes companies are required to value their assets at market prices and reflect in their value their declining life span. Therefore an annual charge is registered in the income statement which is not accompanied by a cash payment. As a result although the actual cash earned may have increased year over year the non-cash charges could result in a reported loss.

The stock market, noting the ongoing reported losing trend, had marked the price of the shares down to a deep discount from book value (the value of the company after deducting liabilities from assets). The book value per share was calculated by dividing the book value by the number of shares outstanding. When the gross book value remained relatively constant and the number of shares decreased the amount resulting from dividing constant book value by a smaller number of shares each year gave a greater value per share. When the company eventually turned around there were fewer shares to divide the corporate earnings by[22] so as to calculate earnings per share and fewer shares over which to spread the dividend pool. The price of the company's shares soared on higher earnings per share than expected and the dividends were reinstituted at a higher level.

That was a piece of financial engineering that proved very beneficial for the shareholders. The only question that arises is; was it undertaken for the benefit of the shareholders or the managers? Many years ago it was decided in the boardrooms of America that if the aims of the managers were aligned with those of the shareholders then a perfect marriage could be concluded. That alignment was obtained by making the managers shareholders. Even if management did not have shareholdings if they were provided with the opportunity to buy the shares at a fixed price then they would become shareholders and benefit as did the public shareholders from corporate stellar performance. It was the birth of management share options. Managers were given, with their annual bonuses, options to buy their employer's shares at a premium of around 10 percent to current market price. The options were time limited to usually

---

22   Note that while it was reporting losses that if the amount of loss stayed constant and the number of shares decreased the loss per share would increase thus putting even more pressure on the share price.

a maximum of five years. If the share price remained constant over the five years there would be no benefit to exercising the option to buy shares from the corporate treasury as the price would be 10 percent higher than the market price. However, if the managers put their shoulders to the wheel and noses to the grindstone and any other contortions that would make the company profitable and thus its shares more valuable they would be financial winners.

The problem with the system was that it aligned the managers with the progress of the share price, not the company. Irrespective of what the long term outcome of their actions might be many mangers took short term pursuits that were only effective in raising the share price. The curse of unintended consequences had struck again. An example would be if you looked at your house and concluded that new curtains would make it more attractive. You decided that rather than repair the leaky basement you chose to install some very attractive curtains. Once installed, you call your local realtor and ask him to appraise your house. He provides an increased valuation and being pleased that such a minor action could be so beneficial, you decide that more such cosmetic actions would be effective in increasing your property's price. The curtains are followed by a fence (another higher appraisal), new landscaping (an even higher appraisal) and a number of other cosmetic activities that from the outside have made the property beautiful. When you have the house viewed by a prospective buyer he notices the damp basement with its cracked concrete and leaking walls and he immediately knocks 30 percent of the value the realtor proposed based on the cosmetics. What you had accomplished was to manipulate the price of your house and not its value. When it came to buy, value trumped price. Very similar outcomes have resulted from short term stock price enhancing pursuits by managers. Some might say that this was the sort of train of events that wrecked "Research In Motion".

A recent court case involved Nortel and its managers who had used accounting reserves to boost the share price to be able to cash in their share options. This occurred while the company was spiraling into insolvency. The earnings were cosmetically enhanced to boost the share price to reward the managers who then exercised their options.

But getting back to share buy backs, they do make sense if the company's share price is overly depressed and management has concluded that the price is unrealistic. To some observers the buyback is an admission that the company's future has dimmed and the outcome will be the eventual end of operations. This is not a tragedy. As I mentioned, many of the component companies of the Dow Jones Index have disappeared. The components of the Dow have been changed as industries have died. Who needs "National Leather" today? The company's time has come and gone and if the directors were honest they would have paid off whatever debts existed and returned the capital to the shareholders through share buy backs and then closed the doors. If they were egomaniacal they would have looked around for a takeover candidate to squander the shareholder's capital and be able to retain their positions and privileges.

There is another situation that can give rise to share buy backs. If there is a controlling shareholder who believes that either her control position has to be enhanced or that the company should be taken private (that is converted from public to private shareholdings) she can achieve this by buying back stock. The need to increase control over the company's ownership often arises when the controlling shareholder believes that her company is a takeover target. A profitable company with dispersed ownership is an easy candidate for a takeover by another corporation, hedge fund or venture capital firm.

The effect of buy backs is to decrease the number of shares in circulation and hence making them more valuable, as I mentioned there are now fewer shares over which to spread the earnings and assets. If the market is rational that should be reflected in the share price because higher value should demand a higher price[23]. If at some point in time the market acts rationally the price will rise and some of the remaining shareholders will capture a capital gain by selling their shares. In most jurisdictions the capital gain will be given preferential tax treatment over dividends. What better way to reward your shareholders than to give them a tax enhanced income?

A share buyback program can be undertaken for a myriad of reasons, some good others bad; however in the end you are the beneficiary. If every year you can sell some of your shareholding at ever increasing prices and you know the buyback will remain in place, then enjoy it.

---

23   This is not always the case as the stock market is emotional rather than rational being run by men and to paraphrase Oscar Wilde, "a speculator is a man who knows the price of everything and the value of nothing".

One Woman One Vote

The above is true in politics but regrettably not in shareholder democracy. Ostensibly you have as many votes as you have common shares in a company. This is true. But what do the votes entitle you to? To begin with you may vote on whether you accept the proffered board of directors at the forthcoming annual meeting. If you feel that the existing board of directors has done nothing to protect the shareholder's interests you only have the option of accepting or rejecting the board. The shareholders can vote 99 percent to reject the board and it would still be accepted because there is no other alternative board to vote for. If you wanted someone on the board that you felt would make a valuable contribution you would have to engage in a costly legal proxy fight to even get the lady's name on the ballot.

This mechanism has meant that there is no real shareholder democracy. Once a group gets control of a board it will be continued to be stuffed with cronies and "yes" men irrespective of the needs of the company. In recent years boards have agreed to unconscionable executive pay when the corporation does well and increases in those amounts even if the company does poorly. As a result companies have been encouraged to add to their annual mailings to shareholders a "say on pay" ballot which of course is non-binding.

To be sure that the insiders of a corporation can continue to reward themselves ostentatiously some companies have set up multiple voting shares. These shares are structured such that one share may have 100 votes compared to your one vote. The very first question that should enter your mind is why would someone find it necessary to do such a thing? The answer is obvious. They are afraid if their actions are too egregious then a one share one vote model could lead to a wreck of their gravy train. Companies with multiple voting shares are now rejected as possible candidates for investment by many pension funds. You should probably accept this as a good guideline.

Another undemocratic approach to corporate governance is the annual mailing to shareholders which provides the opportunity of voting for an entire slate of directors. You either accept the entire slate or reject it. There is no capability to pick or choose amongst the various candidates. If the slate presented to you included Kleptis and Warren Buffet you have to accept both or none.

When, as a young financial analyst I asked a stock salesman what was the answer to this problem he responded that the shareholders could always vote with their feet. By this he meant that if shareholders felt the company was being managed for the benefit of the managers rather than the shareholders they could sell their stock. Obviously if too many shareholders take this approach the share price will languish and if this happens the company could become the object of a takeover by any number of entities such as competitors, venture funds and opportunists. If this occurred the directors might get replaced by a new board and the perks diminished.

Some years ago in Canada there was a gentleman who would buy one share of stock in a company he believed management to be too incompetent or self-serving and attend its annual meeting. He was the Don Quixote of Canadian capitalism in that although his hectoring informed the shareholders of their boards inappropriate behavior there was nothing that could be done.

Some of these undemocratic forms of corporate governance may change in time as pension funds, which have a fiduciary obligation to protect their members, are now starting to become active in bringing errant corporations into behavior that benefits the shareholders. The problem is that these white knights have no real recourse except the courts and that is expensive.

You might think that the market regulators such as the Ontario Securities Commission might be interested in some changes for the benefit of the shareholders to bring about a more democratic regime. The Commission is in place to enforce the Ontario Securities Act which has as its two objectives the protection of investors and the enforcement of free and fair markets. It would seem that shareholder democracy would fall into the realm of investor protection. The Ontario Securities Commission has instead embarked on a path of social engineering by trying to bring about more women on corporate boards. This, although noble, won't protect investors and bring about fair and free markets. Don't expect regulators to take actions to help your investment returns or bring about shareholder democracy.

I have shown you most of the structural snares and traps that await you in the corporate investment market and as concerned as you may be you still have to look after the funds you have to invest. The question on many investor's minds is what is the value of those funds? Is cash king?

The Golden Rule

I am sure you know that rule. It goes as follows:

He who has the gold makes the rules.

If you've got wealth you call the shots.

The rule drives from the fact that there is a very strong belief that the only real money is gold. How did this odd belief come about?

It all started with silver. In 1,000 BC the Athenians began mining silver at Lavrion in Greece. They used that metal to mint a coin called the drachma. The silver was so plentiful that there were enough coins produced to allow the known world to use them as currency. It didn't matter if you were in Assyria or Persia you could transact business in drachmas. However, in 420 BC the Athenians were involved in a bitter war with the Spartans and they began to debase the drachma to pay for the war. The Athenian Government added more and more copper to the silver drachma so that it eventually ended up as a copper coin with silver plating. This allowed the production of more coins with the same starting amount of silver.

As this was happening in Southern Greece there had been significant gold deposits found in the Northern Greek Kingdom of Macedonia. The new gold coins replaced the silver as the world's reserve currency because their value was constant and it was difficult to debase the coins. Any tampering with the coins would be easily discernable. All you had to do was bite it to see how soft it was. There were few gold deposits suitable for mining in the ancient world so there was not a flood of new money coming into the world's economy. In fact there was a shortage of easily extractable gold and bankers began issuing "script" which was a paper note backed by an amount of gold or silver. The final manifestation of this was the US dollar which until August 1970 represented one 35th of an ounce of gold and was exchangeable into that at the US Treasury. The US five dollar bill was actually a "silver certificate" convertible into four ounces of silver.

With all that history you can see that anyone looking at gold and silver thinks of the metals as money. The closing of the US Treasury Gold Window in 1970 heralded the efforts of the world's governments to end the curse of this view and of the monetary "Gold Standard" and the straight jacket it imposed. The US kicked off the campaign to be able to pay for its war in Viet Nam. They had to debase their currency to pay for belligerence in the same way the Athenians had done 2,300 years earlier.

The Gold Standard ties the hands of government to be able to issue currency. Remove the precious metals backing and you can print all the money you want. As soon as the citizenry see the printing presses turned on to print more paper currency they rush to the gold market[24]. If your "paper" is going to double in volume then an ounce of gold will cost you twice as much. Why not buy it today and sell it for twice as much paper in the future?

---

24 I knew a clever investment manager in the early 2000's who, when sensing that the world governments were turning to inflation to pay their bills, bought shares in a company that manufactured bank note paper on which the currencies were printed. He tripled his money in the stock as their earnings climbed.

That describes gold and silver. They are both hedges against currency debasement. They can never be seen as investments as they earn no income, pay no interest or dividends and do not increase in value. Yes they increase in price but not in value. Over time people have devised their own valuations of gold. One yard stick I have heard is that an ounce of gold should buy you one week's of work from a tradesman. For a Canadian tradesman at this time you would need to pay about $40.00 an hour which translates into $1,600 Canadian dollars which is US dollars $1,250 or near to today's price of US $1,300 per ounce. Another historical rule of thumb is that it takes 30 barrels of oil to buy one ounce of gold which at today's price is about US $1,440.

When investors see the cost of a plumber rising unexpectedly or the price of oil rising irrespective of demand they begin to look for inflation. If they find it they have to protect from it and that involves having gold in their portfolios. However, one cannot go on line and grab a few ounces of gold for the online investment account because it is not on offer. Most investors satisfy their need for gold by purchasing gold shares. This is an indirect participation in the gold market but it is convenient.

Where some investor make a mistake is that they think they can invest in gold shares. A gold share is a participation in a gold mine. What is a mine? It is an underground inventory of metal which when extracted and sold will mean the end of the company. Does that sound like a great business model? The companies will tout the fact that they will survive to eternity because they will successfully replace the removed inventory through exploration. As I mention elsewhere in this book your chances of success in mining exploration are 144 to 1. History has shown that when gold companies come to the realization of their mortality they decide to explore or acquire reserves. They may also decide to diversify into other businesses realizing the truth about their own industry. In the majority of cases these efforts have turned into disasters. Yes, seeing inflation looming on the horizon buy your gold shares but on the day you buy them pick your sale price.

There will someday be an international internet based currency. As this is being written there is available "Bitcoin" which although an electronic, net based currency only has the value people attribute to it. At one time speculators attributed a value of $20 to a bitcoin and subsequently $1,000. What is its value? What you believe it is. Is that a viable currency? No.

The currency of the future will be an electronic unit backed by a real asset, probably gold. When you acquire you electronic unit of currency you will know that you can immediately demand from the treasurer of the currency a specific amount of gold. The ability to issue currency will depend on the amount of gold available to back it. Inflation of the gold electronic currency will be impossible.

This may not happen in our lifetimes as governments are used to using inflation to rinse way their debts will fight the adoption of a worldwide stable currency. It will be the Uber and Airbnb fight all over again.

Mummy, Where Do Stock Brokers Come From?

I am not sure if you were asked that question but it is a relevant one. In my experience there does not seem to be the biblical lineage progression such as Stockbroker begat Stockbroker II, who in turn begat Stockbroker III. It seems to be a profession that people drift into. Although there are courses in finance at universities these are more oriented to becoming adept at assessing the value of investments from a corporate point of view rather than the individual investor's. As a result most education for the profession is provided by the investment industry through organizations it has established. When an individual becomes a retail stockbroker what is the penultimate position he can obtain, president of Merrill Lynch or RB Dominion Securities? Not likely. Those jobs usually go to someone in investment banking or trading where the impact of the individual's great accomplishment can be observed and recognition granted. The generating of a million dollars in retail commissions in one year by a retail broker might get him a congratulatory letter from his sales manager and a bigger piece of the commission dollar but he won't be celebrated in the same way as the guy who did the billion dollar deal which will be a road map to the corner office.

So what can the retail stockbroker aspire to? If he is an exceptional performer, generating loads of commission dollars, it would be stupid to put him in management where he could no longer do that. The great performer will be kept in the traces and he knows it. He has a franchise the same as the guy at Tim Hortons or Starbucks. The great stockbroker can only aspire to grow his franchise or "book" as it is known in the trade and maximize the return from his book. His problem is that the service he is offering is the same as everybody else's in the business. Unlike the coffee shop franchiser he can't claim superiority of his service or product over that of his competitors as it does not exist. Buying 100 shares of Bank of Montreal is the same no matter who does it for you. Then why does one become a stockbroker? As one broker pointed out to me, "It's inside work with no heavy lifting". Next, of course, is how does one become a stock broker?

The first step is to convince an investment firm that you have enough contacts to be able to build a "book" and the intelligence to do so. If the sales manager of the firm is convinced, you then start out as a trainee.

The training is rigorous and the student comes out with an understanding of most if not all the measurements of corporate profitability and the benefits from various types of investments. The neophytes also learn how to design portfolios to fit client's needs and financial profiles. Most if not all jurisdictions have a "Know Your Client" rule which in more innocent times meant to know the investment objectives of the client so as to be able to tailor their investments to their financial objectives. In more recent times it includes knowing if the client is engaged in money laundering or other nefarious undertakings. To make sure all is going well the firm will have a "Compliance Officer" whose job it is to insure that the client's portfolio has the right mix of recommended securities to match her risk profile and that she is not funneling money to the Afghan Insurgents[25]. As well, the compliance department will insure that all the regulatory criteria are being obeyed.

Seeing as the broker cannot be calling his clients and maintaining an ongoing program of investment research at the same time, the firm assists him by hiring financial analysts. These people, in the good old days, came from industry. Therefore, if you wanted an analyst to examine the mining industry and the companies involved in it, you hired a geologist or mining engineer with some years of experience in the field. This individual would then take the three year financial analysts course and if he passed all the exams would be given a charter and labeled a "Chartered Financial Analyst" or C.F.A. In earlier times this was a potent combination, a person who had practical knowledge of an industry as well as an understanding of finance. More recent practice has been to take keen young people out of university and give them an industry to follow once they have their C.F.A. charter. The C.F.A. Institute has morphed into more of a degree mill and the rigors of the past education diluted[26].

These analysts will study the industry they're assigned and then find the best investments in that industry. They write extensive reports validating their recommendations which are almost always a buy[27]. The reasons are twofold. Firstly, if the analyst writes a sell recommendation the broker can only voice that to clients already owning the shares whereas a buy can broadcast loud and far, even to those currently owning the stock who could buy more. Secondly, if the executives of a corporation hear of a sell recommendation for

---

25 Although during the Russian occupation of Afghanistan this may have been encouraged.

26 When I obtained my charter as a C.F.A. the organization was run by investment professionals out of the University of Virginia. Their "Institute of Chartered Financial Analysts " has been replaced by a business as the founders died off.

27 In the year 2006 only 6 percent of investment recommendations were sells. The stock markets remained in decline irrespective of the buoyant attitude of the analysts.

their company's shares, the broker issuing that recommendation will be excluded from any future corporate finance business such as new share or bond issues for the company. Needless to say, sell recommendations, even regarding failing companies, seldom if ever reach the level of ten percent of all recommendations. At best failing companies will be "downgraded" to a "hold" but rarely if ever to a sell.

The target market of most investment research is the "institutional" market. This consists of large portfolios held by mutual funds, insurance companies and pension plans. The result is that the companies being researched and written about are those with enough stock in circulation, liquidity, to allow the large funds to participate. If an analyst were to write about a company with a glowing future but only 5 million shares issued few if any institutional investor would be able to buy a meaningful sized participation in the company without distorting the share price. Also, the investment firm is not interested in paying for an analyst who writes a report that might only generate 100 transactions before the shares are overpriced.

If you are hoping for a recommendation about a small start-up pharmaceutical company which has developed the elixir to cure family break up and divorce, you won't find it in the material on offer from your broker's research department. On the other hand if your broker is a hardworking, client oriented individual she might find that company, research it herself and present it to you. I am sure that by now you have noticed the most prevalent word in this chapter is "recommendation". There is a reason for this.

When you receive a call from your registered representative, stock broker, advisor or customers man (the names are interchangeable) he will make a recommendation of an investment for you to buy or sell. He is not going to make that investment decision but will instead give you reasons for you to make that decision. This is important because if the broker makes the decision then he must take some responsibility for it. If you make the decision to act on his information and buy the shares and their price goes into free fall then you are at fault for having bought that "dog". The broker did not decide to buy the "dog", you did. You were not beholden to act on his advice but only to consider it. You made a wrong decision, that is your fault and you can't sue the broker if all the advice he gave you was ill founded and you are now living in penury.

You may well ask why is this financial advisor, registered representative but not stock broker[28], going to all this trouble in calling and advising me? She wants the benefit derived from the commission for buying or selling a security on your behalf. For this she is paid a portion of somewhere between 40 and 60 percent of what the firm charged you to do the transaction. So it matters not one iota if the investment purchased for you goes up or down, the broker and the firm make money.

Now let's assume that you have a highly ethical broker who designs the ultimate portfolio for you and decides that there is no need to interfere with it as it will achieve your needs over the next 5 years. If she has done that for the majority of her clients she will do few if any trades for five years on the exchange and will soon receive a call from her office manager. He will remind her of the firm's threshold of some figure, say $500,000 in annual gross commission, which if not achieved will result in her desk being moved out of the office and on to the curb. The advisor is an investment or asset owned by the brokerage firm. She is like one of Sophia's goats in that she has to provide a return on the investment made in her. If she does not produce she, will not like Sophia's goat find herself on a spit over hot coals but she will be de-hired. If the lady sticks to her principles she will be out of a job and you will hear the dulcet

---

28 A broker is a person who buys something from you and then attempts to sell it for his profit and benefit. Current stock brokers working for investment firms are not real brokers as they act as agents and buy and sell on your behalf.

tones of a new adviser on the phone line. This lady will explain why the bank stock you own should be exchanged for the shares of a different bank (two commissions earned), the telephone utility you own is not as good as the one she is recommending (another two commissions) and how you should swap your pipeline shares for the ones she finds to be better than your current holding (two more commissions).

I have met and observed a number of stellar retail stockbrokers in my career. They are hardworking people who comb the economic, industrial and commercial journals to determine first if their clients should be in shares, next what industries offer the best opportunities and thirdly which companies best represent those industries. Where can I find one of these people, you may ask?

A few years back I met one in the Barcelona harbor living on a sailboat. He had retired at age 45 to join a choir singing Bach cantatas. The pressure of all those about him to look after their needs finally drove him out of the industry and out of Canada. Another individual was so successful that he built an enormous client "book". To efficiently manage that book he had his clients give him discretion over their accounts so that he invested directly for them. He did not charge them a management fee, only commission. The regulators determined that he was unfairly competing with the mutual fund industry and forced him to form a fund which of course increased his costs and brought his investment strategy to light. This did wonders for the existing investment industry but brought no benefits to his clients but rather only increased costs. Those were extreme cases. Usually what happens is a great retail stockbroker is recognized by the professional investors such as mutual and pension funds who then hire them.

What happens if your really good advisor gets hired away and is replaced by his firm with a really bad advisor who has brought you a consistent stream of losers? Let's say she has given 15 duds out of 20 recommendations. The companies cut their dividends or went broke. It sure sounds like incompetence. Regrettably, you can't sue your new advisor for as I pointed out, your advisor did not buy the shares for you. It was you who placed the order.

What defines a good stockbroker; her ability to continuously have your money working for you. What that means is to constantly provide you returns of 10 percent including inflation and 6 percent excluding inflation on an ongoing basis. In other words you want her to match the market long term returns. One of the tools to achieve this is to keep your trading costs down by minimizing the number of transactions as each one of those takes money out of your account. This would mean her acting contrary to her employer's needs. What to do if this isn't happening?

Well you can always fire your stock broker[29].

---

29 One wag commented that the only way to make a killing in the stock market was by shooting a broker.

Going Naked

Without an advisor you are going to be forced into making investment decisions based on your own research and then transacting them or having someone take over the entire investment process for you. Let's look at the latter alternative.

Many years ago an advisor realizing that he was buying all the same shares for each of his many clients and that the portfolios were very similar decided to pool all of his accounts and call them a "mutual fund" in North America or "unit trusts" in the U.K. There were a number of efficiencies to be achieved. By buying shares on the exchange in large 100,000 share lots and distributing them amongst his clients he could minimize his commission costs, the administration costs were reduced and his research costs eliminated. The elimination of research costs occurred because the investment houses seeking his business would send him their research with the understanding that the fund manager would place his orders for shares through the broker offering the research if acted upon.

The mutual funds that originated from this undertaking were like sausages. The final product was just a length of intestine stuffed with pieces from a carcass. In the case of the mutual fund the carcass was the corporate steer. There would be shares of telecommunications, banks, utilities and whatever else the fund manager might find appetizing. Different fund managers had different tastes and so the performance of the funds, like the taste of sausages, was seldom identical. When you go to your butcher and buy some sausages he will price them on what he has inserted in them. Hence you know when you pay by the pound that you should be getting reasonable value. But wait a moment, when it comes time to fry the delicacy you notice that there is way too much inedible fat accumulating in the frying pan. That, madam, is the management fee. The fund operator is not going to provide his services for free. He has to read the research and do the trading and for this the average fund manager in Canada charges between two and three percent of the value of the fund. This is called the "management expense ratio" often referred to as MER. The MER is charged on an ongoing basis. If you had bought all the same shares the fund did and left them in your account you would be more than two percent richer every year having not had to pay the mutual fund's ongoing fees. It gets worse.

In North America 75 percent of the fund managers fail to beat the index they are measured against. In other words if you bought a fund that was invested in US securities the fund would likely underperform either the New York Stock Exchange, Standard and Poor's or the Dow Jones indices. The two major hurdles the fund manager has to overcome are the MER and the funding of redemptions. The MER we have discussed as a value diminishing process but what about redemptions? These were mentioned in the chapter entitled "Sausages" in that a mutual fund guarantees its holders, that upon presentation it will buy the fund units from the holder at a price reflecting the value of the shares constituting the fund at that time. Therefore, a small amount of money has to be set aside so that on any one day the fund can pay for redemptions.

There is as well "index mirroring". One fund manager once described his profession as living in a fish bowl. If you did the same as everybody else you didn't stick out and hence would have your job in perpetuity. Therefore, if the funds under your management mirrored the index you were measured against, you would never do better or worse than the index and hence come under scrutiny. Many fund managers start out with the intention of outperforming the indices and hence becoming masters of the universe. However, as one old veteran of the market mayhem said to me, "the market will do that which discomforts the most participants the most". The young stalwart fund manager having had his head served back to him on a platter will conclude that there is safety in having his portfolio resemble, if not duplicate, the index being his yardstick. The only negative is that he will slightly under perform the index because of the management fee.

Occasionally the financial press will trumpet the outperformance of "active" fund managers by which they mean managers who step outside the index box and find shares that will do better than the index. These individuals do exist and their fund performance will be better than their peers – for a time. However eventually the "efficient market" comes to bear and the golden haired Madonna of the market will find herself back down to earth. The efficient market thesis says that the movement of share prices is random because everything knowable about a company, including the future, is known and reflected in the share price. Over the long term this has proven to be correct in that there are no wealthy portfolio managers, only lucky ones and luck is random. Even investors who claim to not believe the efficient market thesis are in fact believers because every day they go to the market and trade shares at what they believe are correct prices thus believing the market's efficiency. The end result is mutual funds that in most cases mimic an index.

I can see your mind racing ahead to the question, "If he can mimic the index, why can't I"? Of course you can. You could open an account with an advisor or on-line and invest your savings such that your holdings consisted of the shares making up the Toronto Stock Exchange index. Too late, someone has already done that and made the product available on the exchanges. The first entrant to that market was a gentlemen, John Bogle, who set up the Vanguard group of mutual funds that were specifically designed to mirror an index and charge a minimal fee. That was followed by exchange traded funds which closely track the indices. You can buy an exchange traded fund (ETF) that is a mirror image of an exchange index. These go by the exotic names of "Spyders" and "Diamonds" just to name a couple. Therefore depending on what exchange you wanted to mimic you can find a fund that is traded on an exchange that will do just that. Even better, they have minimal management fees usually less than 0.8 percent.

If you were to take the approach of buying an index fund or ETF to hold your retirement income you would never do better or worse than the index. That means over the long term (and Lord Keynes, the eminent economist, said, "in the long term we are all dead') you will achieve a return on investment of 6.1 percent in real terms (after inflation). That 6.1 percent figure derives from the performance of the American markets from the end of the Civil War to today. But within that there was the great depression. If you had bought the bellwether company of the era, United States Steel, in 1928 you would not have gotten your money back until 1956 and that is measured in nominal dollars not counting for inflation. As I write this (2015) the Dow Jones Index is lower than it was at the time of the 2001 attacks on the Twin Towers. If you had bought an ETF mirroring any of the indices in 2001 you would not have seen any growth in your funds to today. You would be richer because during that time you would have received dividends. Although the value of your shareholdings has not substantially changed, your cash position in the account would be higher. I hope this has put aside any thoughts you may have had that the stock market would be your source of infinite riches. Read what the words say, it is a market where people come to sell their stocks and buy others, it is an exchange. There is nothing in that to make you believe that this is your path to wealth. Investments are savings – end of story.

We are better than half way through this discourse and what I hope I have done thus far is warn you of the pitfalls. You may well ask, "If these are all the pitfalls, is there any hope?" Yes there is. The stock market can produce reasonable returns; note I didn't say gains, over the life time of your investment. Think back to Sophia and Dimitri. What if for ten years the value of their goats and orchards remained constant as the stock market value has in the most recent decade? The couple would have every year sold the output from their assets and likely bought more assets, even in the stagnant or depressed market for farm properties in Athens at that time. Although the value of their assets had not increased they would be richer as the amount of assets they owned had increased. Even if they sold all their accumulated assets at the end of their working lives for what they had paid for them they would still be richer than 30 years earlier when they first started working the farm. But don't forget Kleptis.

Assuming you are going into the investment swamp alone it may be best to tell you of some of the ways of the professionals.

Working in Her Shoes

You may wonder how the portfolio manager for a mutual fund makes a decision when confronted with all the available shares and information about them. It is a daunting task.

At the start of the day she will review the market's actions of the past day, the economic news and then the political news. She is now up to date on the current state of the investment markets and their environment but as an active manager she has to be cognizant of how her portfolio fits into today's environment. Does her portfolio reflect the possible war tensions rising in the Middle East? What shares should she own if the situation escalates? What about the economic boom in Asia? Will it change the pricing of mineral commodities in North America? Will the shares of mining and oil companies reflect this or has it already happened?

As you can see there is information overload. This is one of the many reasons that an increasing number of portfolio managers become closet indexers that structure their portfolios to reflect the index against which they are measured. Their problem is that their performance relative to their index is measured quarterly. A couple of bad quarters and she could find herself unemployed. What I discovered while in the industry was that mutual fund managers were forced into a no win situation for their clients. The constant need to own the darling of this calendar quarter was more difficult than keeping up with the fashion dictates of Vogue Magazine. Like dress fashions, it was impossible to get ahead of the curve. Like dress fashion there was a cost in being fashionable and for the portfolio manager it was the trading costs incurred in buying and selling shares from her portfolio.

There was a group of professional money managers who I envied as they had a much better industry life. These were the people who managed money for private clients whether pension funds, trusts or individuals. A number of them I would call on had an interesting rule. "Give me the three top reasons I should own this company's shares or bonds."

By invoking this rule the money manager had only to know the three major criteria that were controlling the share price and what to be aware of. I remember visiting a private portfolio manager in New York with an interesting thesis on why he should invest in Tyco Industries bonds which had seen their price destroyed by the activities of the company's CEO and his purchase of a $6,000 shower curtain for his mistress at the company's expense. When I walked into his office he said, "I don't want to hear about the bloody shower curtain and what it means to the corporate culture, attitudes within the company and weakness in the board." I replied, "Shower curtain? What shower curtain? I am here to talk about the Tyco subsidiary that is going to double its earnings in three years and they're not in the shower curtain business."

I gave him the most important three reasons to own the bonds. When I arrived at our offices there was an order for $5 million of the Tyco bonds at the market offered price.

Another private funds manager had a simple rule. He only held ten different shares in his portfolio. His reasoning was he had eliminated 85 percent of the risk of owning only one share and he did not want the strain of having to consider the prospects of a large number of varied companies. To get him to act on my recommendation

I had to show him why the company I was proposing was better than his number ten. Some 40 years ago I asked Freddy what his number ten was to which he replied, Bally, the manufacturer of arcade games that was entering the slot machine business. I needed only to show Freddy that the markets were aware of the company's outlook and the limits to which the casino business could expand. That compared to my uranium company which was in an industry with an undisclosed shortage of the commodity was an easy sell. When a year later the uranium shortage was discovered the shares of Denison Mines tripled.

A system that has shown better than average result has been around for a long time and it involves buying shares or increasing positions in currently held shares on certain calendar dates. You could decide to buy on the 15th of January, March, June, September and December a pre-ordained dollar amount of shares or bonds. The method is a tried and true procedure going back decades and is called "Dollar Averaging". The method has been examined by many researchers and found to produce roughly an annual average return about 30 percent higher than you might expect from a passive portfolio over half a century. Therefore, if your passive portfolio could be expected to provide you with a ten percent return on average (including inflation) over half a century, your dollar averaging portfolio would provide you closer to 13 percent. You could not defer your buying because the market was too high or low. The day has arrived and your fixed amount of funds must be invested. This works well because of the "Random Walk Down Wall Street" thesis. Without being influenced by the state of the market you make your investment. You will find that on the occasion you would have considered deferring because the market seemed overpriced that it continued to become even more overpriced. Likewise fearing that the market was in free fall you might have otherwise deferred buying more shares only to find that shortly thereafter the market had turned around. Dollar averaging requires no research and a lot of discipline.

A variation of dollar averaging is "Value Averaging" Where instead of investing a fixed amount on a fixed date you invest more when the market is depressed and less when it is in a roaring bull phase. The problem is who is to determine whether the market is in a continuing rising phase or whether it is to continue to be depressed as it was for the first decade of the 2000's?

Another portfolio tool I saw often applied by the professionals involved her walking into her office in the morning and reviewing her portfolio. She would then ask herself the question, "Would I buy all of these holdings today?" If she found any of her positions as not what today's circumstance would describe as a buy then she sold them. For this portfolio manager there is no "hold", a share is either a buy or a sell.

As well as the simplicity of these investment approaches, note the discipline. Too many professional investors get caught up in the fashion page also known as the "business news". They are continuously pursuing the hot new idea while not understanding that if it is in the press it is already in the price of the shares.

Those criteria stuck with me and I used some of them myself with some success. However, what is important in investing is to have rules and be disciplined enough to follow them. It is even more amazing to consider how simple ideas triumph. Most market participants are not interested in simplicity.

Look carefully at the business press. The airwaves and pages are full of opinions as to when to buy and sell shares. There are seldom investment recommendations but instead purchases of shares with a "target" sell price. How does the guru know that the share will achieve that price as the price is more determined by the attitudes in the market place than the company's attributes. When the shares achieve that "target" price how does the guru know that the event occurred as a result of his brilliant insight or the buoyancy of the market at the time?

To go back to the real estate investment, when you bought the investment property was it with a sell price objective or to earn an income? The same should apply to your stock market investing otherwise you are not investing, you are speculating.

You can't go wrong!

Sort of. There are so many snares and traps in investor land that I wonder why so few are ever exposed. Even before you begin to worry if you have a safe and prosperous portfolio you may be subjected to any number of prospective offers which are pure swindles.

The most common is the Ponzi scheme (also sometimes called government services). This type of swindle involves taking funds from current investors to pay earlier investors (government pension schemes being typical). It was first devised by Charles Ponzi, in Boston. He claimed that by exploiting the differences in the pricing of postal products he could generate spectacular investment returns. As word spread of his success in paying investors large returns, new investors gave him more money with which to pay past investors their high returns, however, this kind of plan only works as long as the number of participants continues to expand. When the number of new entrants could not supply the funds promised to the prior entrants the scheme collapsed and Ponzi was jailed. When the number of new entrants to the work force falls, the government funding for current pension and health schemes is reduced. I am sure that this has answered a question that has long burdened you, "Why is the government so focused on immigration?" The immigrants are the new entrants to the Ponzi scheme.

As I mentioned, the majority of government schemes are un-funded in that money has not been put aside to pay for the benefits promised and the system works only as long as more entrants are heading for the workforce. If the birth rate falls, as it always does as a country industrializes[30], there will be fewer new entrants to the taxpaying mass that governments are counting on to pay for the benefits promised. Note the principal requirement for a Ponzi or any other swindle is that you have given your capital or wealth to someone or something. Without having your money, the swindler cannot proceed.

You would think that with the well documented and understood concept of the Ponzi scheme it would be nigh impossible to perpetrate today, yet in 2008, it was revealed that Bernard Madoff (a onetime president of the NASDAQ Exchange) had executed a perfect Ponzi operation to the extent of $65 Billion for more than several decades. Madoff's scheme was a classical application of Ponzi's methods although most modern schemes have some variation in their execution. The one thing they all have in common is the promise of high returns. Their guarantee of success in the first instance results from human greed.

The giveaway for a Ponzi scheme is the promise of exceptional investment returns. Remember when we said that the market was efficient in that the price of securities was based on the fact that all that could be known about the underlying company was common knowledge, therefore, no one could have an advantage. The typical Ponzi scheme makes the claim that the perpetrator has unearthed an inefficiency in the market place. In Charles Ponzi's case he claimed to have found a discrepancy in the pricing of postal products. The

---

30   In agrarian societies children are assets to work the fields and therefore the birth rates are high in those groups. In industrialized societies children are a self-indulgence who have to be fed, clothed and educated and hence a constant drain on the purse. Children are a liability in industrialized societies which is why some of the participants chose to have Porches rather than a babies. You can always sell the Porsche when tired of it.

problem is that this might or not be true. At one time I found that a particular type of security that was of little interest to the either the equity or bond investor as it was a hybrid not fitting into either group's criteria for investment. For a number of years I exploited that inefficiency to great success but like all inefficiencies in the investment market, others will soon discover it and the competition for that product will bring the market into an efficient profile.

So when someone claims that she has found an undiscovered niche, it can have the ring of truth to it. When asked to explain the basis of the money making scheme a fraud perpetrator will either refuse to divulge this as it is a secret or describe it in such an arcane manner as to be unintelligible.

All Ponzi scheme variations have the defining feature of wanting to have control of your money. If the fraudster does not have possession of your assets she can't steal them. The other foil to the success of the Ponzi scheme is to ask the lady in the sincere dark suit and perfectly ironed blouse why she is allowing you to participate in this fantastic money making scheme rather than keeping it all for herself?

Mark Twain once famously remarked that "a gold mine is a hole in the ground with a liar at the other end". He had been in Virginia City for the great gold and silver rush and owned a number of shares in now defunct companies. His problem was that the companies never had any prospect in the first place. But it is not just the mining venture that offers the boiler room[31] operators the opportunity to fleece investors. These fraudsters work on the principle of selling shares in companies that own something that might increase in

---

31 The term "boiler room" stems from a time when the operators of scams would set up their headquarters in the lowest priced real estate available because they never expected to meet their victims and the venture would be short lived. They found that the basements of prestigious office buildings provided good addresses with cheap rents. They therefore rented the boiler room.

value such as real estate, mining claims, oil leases or technology. The essence of a speculation is that no one can ascribe a value to the asset underlying the shares and hence the shares themselves. Who is to know that a piece of land will be rezoned from its current lowly residential status to high density commercial? Or how about the question of how much oil lies beneath an oil lease if any? Remember that as an investor you are buying income producing assets. The barren goat that might yet conceive and produce kids is not for you. You want the animal that is now producing revenue and will continue to do so.

Mark Twain fell prey to the checked suited promoter whose successors work the markets today. They will boast of great discoveries such as the Voisey Bay nickel deposit and the great Hemlo gold find. Their pitch is of the sort that if you had put a dollar into either of those companies when they were trading as junior mines then you would have thirty or forty times your money today. Is that enough of a return for this kind of speculation, no.

The best recorded history of mining exploration was that of the old Cominco Company, owners of the Trail, B.C., smelting complex and the surrounding mines. The company spent $300 million on exploration between the years 1924 and 1964. They examined one thousand properties. Of those they took 68 to advanced exploration, which meant they spent more than $75,000 on the deposit. Of those 68 that went into extensive exploration only seven went into production and made a profit or returned the original investment. What that tells you is that your odds of success in investing in mining exploration are 143 to one (1000/7). You have to make $143 for the one dollar you bet on the winning company to offset the losses on all the failures. Unlike the Cominco Company you do not have a smelter to feed and therefore don't have to take the 143 to one odds.

But then of course along comes the chap with the sincere blue suit and the club tie who will describe to you the great benefits of high tech. The first high tech stock traded in North America was that of a company that could take your message across the continent in the blink of an eye. That company, Western Union, came about in 1848 and its share price went from under ten dollars to almost 50 and then back to under ten dollars all in the space of half a decade.

The next great performer, sort of, was a company that in1923, announced it could place your voice in every household in America once the masses had bought their newfangled device called the radio. The shares of Radio Corporation of America (RCA) went from $10 to $120 and back to $10 again in less time than it took Benny Goodman and Guy Lombardo to get to the top of the music charts.

You now know that the high tech boom and bust is nothing new and you have seen the recent manifestations in the likes of Nortel and RIM.

I don't seem to be doing a good job of telling you how to invest as all I am giving you is warnings of things that could be damaging to your wealth. Is there anything else that I should be aware of, you are asking, yes. In some situations a stock broker can be dangerous to your financial health.

The Dangers of Unprotected Investing

To put this into real context, I know of a lady whose account was taken over by a nice young man with red suspenders after her broker moved on. In the space of one year the nice young man did 47 trades in her account, bought two oil company's shares that were on their way to zero, as well as shares that would double in ten years and units in a real estate partnership that would not be redeemed for five years. This was done in the account of a 68 year old, arthritic widow who doesn't even buy green bananas. When I questioned the compliance officer at the large American broker about the speculative shares his answer was that the widow was wealthy enough to be able to lose some money. I asked what level of wealth I needed to achieve to be able to take advantage of their money losing schemes. He was not forthcoming[32]. The result of all this trading was about $50,000 in commission and a loss of about

---

32 His exact comment was that, "as a professional, you know we can't guarantee investment performance, good or bad".

$2 million in a $5 million account. When I was presented with this information I was appalled. So I took action[33].

My first stop was the Ontario Securities Commission (OSC). This institution was set up to pursue the objectives of the Ontario Securities Act which are to protect the investor and insure orderly markets. The commission was not interested but instead passed the information on to the Investment Industry Regulatory Organization of Canada (IIROC). This is an organization set up by the stock brokers to police stock brokers, sort of like an organization of used car dealers to oversee the action of used car dealers. Needless to say they don't discipline many, in either case. The very thorough investigation by IIROC showed that the registered representative had acted quite professionally in losing over one third of the lady's money by churning her account. However, sensing foul play it instigated an investigation of me for having reported the incident. Later, when it was discovered that I had subsequently obtained the wronged lady a five figure settlement from the broker who had churned her account the alarm bells went off. This award was obtained through the offices of the Ombudsman for Banking and Investment Services (OBSI). The Ontario Securities Commission started an investigation of me and my associates that resulted in my being charged as "unco-operative" and "acting contrary to the public interest". You can't imagine my shame. If I had only known that it was contrary to the public interest to constantly earn double digit returns for widows over a decade and attempt to obtain recompense for them when they are defrauded, I would have immediately desisted and turned myself in to the authorities. However, like the Ontario Securities

---

33 When I reported the incident to the regulators I received a letter indicating that I would be investigated. The investigation lasted 5 years and cost me tens of thousands of dollars. So intent was the OSC on a conviction that their investigator, Larry Masci, created fraudulent documents, and encouraged fraud. The lawyer Jonathon Feasby, presented false documents to a witness he tried to intimidate to sign them and then went on to lie to the Commissioner at the hearing. Yes, these are criminal activities.

Commission, I could not find any evidence that I had violated the Ontario Securities Act. Unable to get a conviction they settled for "it was likely that I advised without being registered" as all their witnesses testified that I had not provided them with investment advice nor had they paid me for advice. Well you might ask, how it is "likely" that someone committed an offence. On the other had I had concrete evidence of fraud by the Ontario Securities Commission. When I tried to lay charges the Attorney General's office and the Ontario Securities Commission colluded to prevent any charges being laid. The Commission didn't want charges heard in court as it was obvious that their employees would be convicted. Therefore they conspired with law enforcement to stop the charges from being heard. What you should learn from this is that you cannot rely on the regulators to protect you. Should you contact the regulators about a perceived infraction they will downplay its severity and discourage you from further inquiry. Should you protest too strenuously you may be pursued and charged with a "likely" violation of the Ontario Securities Act.

I should explain what was done to the lady's portfolio that resulted in her receiving a settlement. Firstly the portfolio was "churned". This means that there was excessive trading in the account. This is exemplified by the buying and selling of shares in which there has been little price movement. Typically this would involve buying, let's say the Bank of Montreal shares at $58.00 per share and selling them at $58.75 to buy Bank of Commerce shares at $76.00 selling those at $77.00 to purchase Bank of Nova Scotia shares and on and on. The client makes very little and the broker a lot.

Then there is "stuffing". This is very similar to what your butcher does with sausages. Your broker takes the bits of the corporate carcass that won't sell and stuffs them into a sausage, your account. Your investment firm having bought a new issue resembling offal and finding that it is not a best seller will look for a place where it can be off loaded from their inventory. Where better to off load it than at an unsophisticated client. For example let's say the investment firm your broker works for has just bought a piece of the supposedly hot new issue of "Almost Useful Technology" and the market reception has been appalling. The brokerage's sales manager will step onto the sales floor and yell to all and sundry that the commission for selling the new issue has been doubled and there will be an "iPod" given to the salesman who has the highest volume of sales in the shares. The salesmen will then look for the least astute of their clients and proclaim the virtues of "Almost Useful Technology" to them and the shares will be placed. The process is called stuffing as the investment offal was unsalable and hence had to be forced into accounts.

You must always be vigilant when working with a registered representative as he is not working for you; he is working for himself and his firm. Your welfare is of no concern to him. His commission cheque is his sole source of income. What makes matters worse is the concept of regulator capture. If you complain to your local regulator[34] about being taken advantage of, the commission will more often than not, blame you and your insatiable greed, for allowing the malfeasance.

What is regulator capture? When in the USA, the Interstate Commerce Commission was set up it, it was meant to protect shippers from rapacious railways. Now it assures the monopolies of the shipping companies. Similarly, the Canadian Radio and Telecommunications Commission, when it was instituted, was to protect Canadians from the telephone monopolies. It now works to increase their profits through internet bandwidth control and limiting cell phone industry entry. Likewise, the Ontario Securities

---

34 In my last book, "Decommissioned" I explain the concept of regulator capture whereby institutions formed to oversee and control enterprises on behalf of the consumer end up supporting the needs of the industry in opposition to the consumer's needs. Think of the CRTC with respect to broadcasters and cell phone users.

Commission, rather than provide the protection for the investor, demanded by the Ontario Securities Act, the Commission acts to protect the industry and its brokers from investors who have been abused.

Why would it do that you may ask? The answer is that a stockbroker or advisor is a very valuable entity. How valuable? The most recent transaction was the sale of 120 stockbrokers by HSBC to National Bank for $2.25 million apiece. The OSC or IIROC is not about to destroy the investment firm's $2.25 million asset over the stuffing of a widow's account. How far will the regulators go to protect the regulated's assets? Let me give you an example.

When RBC Dominion Securities discovered that one of its brokers, Mark Steven Rotstein, along with his associate, Jessica Elisabeth Zackheim, had been forging their client's signatures on documents for a decade they promptly threw them out the door. Scotia Capital seeing a half billion dollar "book" sitting on the street looking for a home just as promptly hired them. IIROC was willing to let the duo continue working in the industry if they would agree to a one year trading suspension to be served over two years in six month segments. In that way one of them would always be available to man the phones while the other stayed home serving their suspension. The duo was also hit with a $250,000 fine for him and $50,000 for her, insignificant amounts when considering that the hiring bonus a broker receives for moving is in the magnitude of millions of dollars. IIROC claimed that no financial harm befell the clients from the forging which then begs the question, why did the perpetrators do it?

IIROC was happy to have the pair working at Scotia as long as any signed documents in client accounts were verified by management and they were also assured by the fact the that the duo had seen the path of virtue and had promised to go "straight" in the future. Regrettably they were like Saint Augustine who said, "Lord make me virtuous, but not yet." The duo went on to be reprimanded again.

What this tells you is that there is no protection for you by regulators and that you should not blindly assume that nice soothing voice on the other end of the phone does not belong to a financial shark.

Some readers will conclude that regulator capture is just a Canadian phenomenon. Not so. In 2008 Lehman Brothers went broke to the extent of $370 billion, a not insignificant sum. Lehman's was the fourth largest bank in the world and at the time of its bankruptcy had employees of the United States Securities Exchange Commission in its offices for a period of months overseeing Lehman's operations and financial reporting. So it would seem logical to assume that the SEC knew what was happening. What was happening was that Lehman's was using false accounting, accounting tricks and outright deceit to keep the regulators appeased. You may well ask, "Wasn't the purpose of the regulators to uncover this sort of thing?" On paper, yes, but in fact the problem that comes up is that in usually less than five years a regulator set up to oversee an industry will be 'captured' by the industry resulting in the regulator working to protect the industry from the citizens.

You would be justified in asking if I can provide concrete proof that the Ontario Securities Commission is acting to protect and advance the investment industry. Yes, I can. Around 2009 the Commission acted to have the Ontario Securities Act changed so that anyone was allowed to act as an advisor as long as it was "not for a business purpose". Can you explain to me why prohibiting your cousin, Broadbrain, from receiving a payment for the investment advice he has provided you protects you, the investor? If he doesn't receive payment are you then protected? That legislation certainly provides protection to "Stuffem and Churnem Securities" your local boiler room securities firm not to mention the big banks as they will no longer have competition from any commercial amateurs, no matter how brilliant.

The Commission may have been motivated by the fear all ossified institutions have of the internet. As the internet sowed havoc amongst the retail trade and destroyed the publishing and book distribution industries, so it will soon destroy the stock brokerage industry as we know it.

The first commissioned stock salesman in Canada was a man by the name of Jarvis who worked at the Greenshields firm. This momentous shift occurred sometime in the mid 1950's. Prior to that the people who managed investor's portfolios were paid by salary. The old style firms knew that a commission driven system could lead to a conflict of interest. The conflict would arise when the salesman would have to consider whether a transaction was being undertaken for the client's benefit or the commission it would earn him. We have moved away from that genteel and honest approach of maximizing the client's wealth to the current situation where the defining strategy is pursuit of the commission dollar. The economics of the situation are quite simple. In a private investment arena the expected return on investment is no less than 15 percent. If an investment firm buys a new broker for $2.25 million dollars the minimum net return they would expect for a year is $337,500 (15% X $2,250,000 investment). If the commission dollars are split 50:50 with the firm and the salesman each receiving half then the total commission generated by the broker can be no less the $675,000 per year to provide each party $337,500. Let's say with overhead the advisor, salesman, broker, whatever you wish to call him, has to generate at least three quarters of a million dollars in commission. The net result is that although your financial advisor has designed for you the ultimate portfolio that should provide you the income you need for the next half decade his sales manager will be able to find fault with it and suggest another trade or eight.

You will often see that before there is a corporate announcement regarding a company, its share trading volumes will increase dramatically. How is it that this trading occurs in the days prior to an announcement? It is a result of insider trading. In other words people who know of the impending news buy or sell the shares in anticipation of the news release. This is called "insider trading" and is illegal. The "smoking gun" is in the trading volume charts prior to the announcement. If the Commission was guaranteeing orderly markets it would prosecute the individuals or firms involved in the insider trading. In the same way that it does not guarantee efficient markets the Commission does not protect the investor as evidenced by the fact that it would not act for the elderly widow I mentioned. When was the last time you heard of a broker being chastised for abusing a client? FAIR, a monitoring organization, noted that in Canada, 78 percent of all frauds perpetrated against investors during the past decade were at the hands of individuals or organizations registered with a securities regulator.

The investment industry has taken heed of the folly of the commission driven investment advisor and some advisors have forsaken that for what the industry is all about – investment performance. This breed will offer you an account that charges you a fee for the investment service. It might be, let's say 0.8 percent annually of the assets under administration. If you place your million dollar RRSP with the advisor she will make $8,000 from you in the first year. But if the RRSP is worth $2 million in 5 years she is now making $16,000 a year from you. Obviously your portfolio manager, advisor or whatever you want to call her, now has her objectives aligned with yours in that you both benefit from the lowest possible trading costs and the best growth. Critics of this system complain that the advisor can make money for doing nothing. If the value of your portfolio is increasing annually what do you care?

The investment industry has recently adopted more thorough reporting from the investment firm to the client in that costs and performance have to be shown in an easily understood fashion. You will now know if your fee based advisor is performing well for you.

There is another structure that does beat the self-serving system and has therefore become more prevalent. Under that system an investor will find a friend or associate with experience in the financial markets. These are retired people usually found missing short putts on golf courses or trying to patch holes in boats in yacht clubs. As well as there being a wealth of information under that sparsely haired pate there is the lack of avarice of the conventional broker or mutual fund firm. If the golf club is tony or the yacht impressive then you can assume that this is not the type of individual to be reckless with money. If you have known the person for a substantial period of time why not ask them to assume the trading authority on your investment account? By appointing them as the attorney on your account with the restriction that they can only buy or sell investments but not be able to move assets in or out of the account you may have the perfect solution to your dilemma. Don't forget that according to the Ontario Securities Act if she does it for free it is legal. For god's sake don't buy her a lunch!.

If the attorney structures your account to mirror theirs then you will have a situation where you do not have to endure phone calls from enthusiastic young brokers trying to convince you to buy something you know nothing about on the basis of knowledge that is meaningless to you. In fact you will probably never hear from your attorney and the only information you will receive is when he or she buys or sells something in your account and of course your monthly statement.

Obviously this mirrors the fee based account but with a greater sense of familiarity.

Let's Go Shopping!

The message I have been giving you so far has been less than thrilling consisting of descriptions of how your fortune, large or small, can be made smaller. Therefore, we should take a break and do something more pleasurable like shopping. So grab your portfolio and let's go to the market.

From the previous chapter you learned that investment dealers, their employees as well as the mutual fund companies are making scads of money in the market. Not by investing, that would be like a dope dealer using cocaine. No the profits come from being able to do business in the stock markets. As the farmer asked when being shown the stock broker's yachts in a New York marina, "Where are the client's yachts?" As I have said on many occasions if you believe in mutual funds buy their shares, that's right, the shares of the companies offering the funds, they will by far outperform the funds they issued. If you think the banks are making a killing from stock market investors, buy their shares. There is something we might consider on our shopping spree.

On any shopping outing the question is what to buy and is it worth it? For your investment shopping I have attempted to steer you away from speculating (buying something to sell to the greater fool) but towards an asset that will pay you a return. The question that arises is what will you earn by holding a basket of securities representing the share markets generally? Research was done by one of the world's largest banks that gave the following results for the world markets.

	Price Change	Dividend Distribution Rate	Total Return	Inflation Rate	Real Price Change	Real Total Return
1950's	13.2 %	5.4%	19.3%	2.2%	10.7%	16.7%
1960's	4.4%	3.3%	7.8%	2.5%	1.8%	5.2%
1970's	1.6%	4.3%	5.8%	7.4%	-5.4%	-1.4%
1980's	12.6%	4.6%	17.3	5.1%	7.1%	11.6%
1990's	15.3%	2.7%	18.1%	2.9%	12.0%	14.7%
2000's	-2.7%	1.8%	1.0%	2.5%	-5.1%	-3.4%
1950 2010	7.2%	3.6%	11.0%	3.8%	3.3%	7.0%

The above table is very important although in looking at the values in any one column alone you would say that there is no pattern or consistency and that the numbers look random. Well that is true, because as previously discussed, the "efficient market thesis" has decreed that the market outcomes are random. As well note that dividends make up more than half of the market return of seven percent over the 60 years shown and are always positive. Over that time you could have said forget about the price of my portfolio just keep sending me the dividends and you would have been an astute investor.

Therefore dividends, or your share of the corporate earnings, are an important part of the growth in your investment. Like Dimitri and Sophia you can accumulate wealth as long as your goats and land are providing a constant source of income. They did not buy the animals and property to have them increase in price; they bought them to get paid a return on their capital. There is the best potential candidate for your portfolio, investments that pay you, a phenomenon I call "getting paid to wait".

In looking at the real growth in the price of stock portfolios note that over the 60 years it has been 3.3 percent or about the same as the average growth in Gross Domestic Product (GDP)[35] of the countries involved. That would seem intuitively correct in that it would be difficult to conceive of the value of a market growing more or less than the country's economy. What we can take away from this is that when we go shopping the only investments that should be attracting our interest are those with a dividend otherwise we are giving up more than half of our potential profit.

Here we are in the market place. I see you've noticed those "puts", "calls", "warrants", currency funds and commodity ETF's being hawked from the isles. Ignore those as they are not real investments. They are akin to the vendors of scarves and trinkets waiting outside the food market. There are only two investments, shares or bonds. Everything else derives from them hence their names, derivatives. The shares we are going to look at are those of the fictional company "Mammoth Industries". As you've learned a share is a proportional ownership in a company. What we need to know about Mammoth before we buy its shares is what they are going to pay us. So we have to find a source from which we can determine the dividend rate. We need a source of information and the internet has provided us with that. There are many sites offered by financial newspapers that will air the dirty linen of the corporation that interests you. Barring that you can enlist the advice of an advisor, stockbroker or investment dealer, whatever you want to call him or her. Here are the questions:

---

35 The Gross Domestic Product is the value of all the goods and services produced by an economic unit such as a country.

- What is the amount of the dividend and how often is it paid?
- How long has this company been paying dividends?
- When was the last increase in the dividend?

We now know the dividend history. The dividend is a portion of the earnings of the company that the directors have decided to pay to the owners. New questions:

- What is the company's 5 year earnings history? What did they earn per share?
- What was the proportion of the earnings that got paid to the shareholders? You can calculate this yourself if mathematically inclined.
- What has been the cash flow per share for the past five years?

Now we know the company's capability to continue paying its owners. In recent years the cash flow being generated by a company has been recognized by many investors as more important to the sustainability of the payouts to investors than the reported earnings number. There are companies that payout more than their reported earnings because they have very high non-cash charges deducted from their earnings calculation such that the actual cash available is in excess of the reported earnings. Accountants will depreciate a company's assets to reflect their increasing age and demand that a charge be made to reflect this, they will insist that funds be put aside for potential liabilities arising out of the company's operations (consider for example pipeline spills) and any other potential liability that can be attributed to this year's operations. Inevitably cash flow is greater than earnings because these 'set asides' diminish the reported earnings figure. Earnings per share can be "managed" or "massaged" to bring them into line with management's presentation needs. Cash flow is the real amount of money that the operations of the company generated and available to pay your dividend or interest.

Well you may ask, "What kind of company or more importantly industry can generate stable continuous cash flow?" If I gave you the opportunity to borrow from me at 5 percent and lend that mount out at 10 percent to your neighbour you would realize that this was an instant source of income. In most economies the interest paid on short term loans is lower than that paid on longer term loans to recognize the risk in having your money in the borrower's hands for a longer term. The whole idea of a financial institution is based on that concept called the 'spread'.

You loan money to your bank by making a deposit. Because that money is immediately available to you in that you can withdraw it without notice the bank pays a pittance in the form of interest. If you are willing to lend the bank on a fixed term basis such as a Guaranteed Investment Certificate or Certificate of Deposit where the bank has your money for a fixed term they will pay you slightly more. The money that the bank borrows short term in the form of deposits it lends out to consumers and corporations on a long term basis at much higher rates. That spread between lending and borrowing is the bank's profit. There are of course other segments to the banks business but that is the basis. Every financial company has this spread concept as the foundation of its income.

I am sure you can see the benefits of being a bank owner just on the basis of that business model which has existed from the time of the Medici's. However, it gets better. As you can see from the business model this is an important segment of the national economy and can never be allowed to fail so this leads to an implicit government guarantee that banks will not fail. They will always work themselves into a position of near death but the government will always bail them out. Your friend Tanya Trader will warn you that unlike other industries the cream does not rise to the top. Consistency wins at the bank but with consistency comes boredom and a belief that if the managers of the bank can do so brilliantly at borrowing short and lending long they are financial geniuses. That hubris will take flight and the managers will strive to get into financial minefields but government is always lurking in the background to save the banks from themselves.

You are justified in asking if there is a history that can verify the investment performance of the banks. If you were to look at the worst performing Canadian bank of the last 20 years it would be the Bank of Montreal which has provided an 8 percent increase in price on average annually. If you include the dividends paid the average annual return to the investor has been almost 13 percent. The best performing bank over the past 20 years has been the Bank of Nova Scotia which provided almost 12 percent price growth and including dividends would have yielded 15 percent. Had you invested $10,000 of your capital in the Bank of Nova Scotia you would have almost $180,000 today. Had you done so you would have been following the Warren Buffet program of buying good companies with a proven market and little competition. Another interesting feature of those boring old bank stocks is they all outperformed the Canadian stock exchange averages over those past 20 years by a factor of at least six times. If you had a financial advisor he or she would have called you over the course of those 20 years, remarking on the fact that you had substantial capital gains in your bank shares and it was now time to move on. The truth is why would you sell a goat that is providing a steady supply of milk and kids? Who is to say that a sheep might be more profitable?

We have obviously found the right isle in the market and one of the best looking products. You can see stacked up next to the bank shares other financial product shares like insurance and mortgage companies all of which operate on that lucrative simple spread model. The other features of these companies are that as well as being protected from foreign competition they are shielded domestically as well by their structure. These businesses require a lot of capital to start and operate and take a long time to establish. These are the kind of things one likes to have in a portfolio. Having purchased some of those let's move on. Why you may comment? I just love these financial shares and their luscious dividends. I want to only own financial shares.

The old saw I mentioned briefly about diversifying has to be addressed. With one share or one industry in your portfolio your exposure to risk is 100 percent to that entity alone. So we should do some more shopping and spread our risk. The question you should ask is, "what if anything resembles those lovely bank and insurance company shares?" Well what about utilities? There is another business where the company is providing a service; it is regulated with a defined income stream and little to spend its money on other than keeping its operations up to date. This is a business model with little or no competition and a government backstop. They would make an excellent second choice as a group. But remember to eliminate the specific risk of owning only one stock or group we need at least ten investments. At this point our portfolio has one bank, one insurance company and one near bank like a mortgage or personal finance lender. Let's add a pipeline and an energy supplier.

Remember I mentioned that you were a reluctant investor. Now you should begin to feel some of the effects of that condition. Here you only have your shopping cart half-filled and you have to buy something less than good like those lovely financials or even the utilities. You are still looking for companies with steady cash flow and a willingness to pay its owners. Shall we take a look at REIT's? REIT's are **R**eal **E**state **I**nvestment Trusts and they look very much like that sausage on offer, the mutual fund units, so much so that they are called units. The idea of a REIT is that a sum of money is raised and then invested in a portfolio of income generating real estate properties. As long as management isn't ripping off the unit holders at the expense trough, these can be nice money makers for the portfolio. Like dividends this income is subject to special tax treatment. Probably members of your family may have said "You can't go wrong owning real estate". To quote Gershwin from Porgy and Bess, "It ain't necessarily so". From 1990 to 1996 the average house price in Canada collapsed 30 percent. In mid-1990's the great commercial real estate companies like Bramalea, Cambridge as well as Olympia and York disappeared. You could have bought shares in any of those commercial real estate companies and would have lost your blouse. The difference is that those commercial real estate companies carried great amounts of debt or "leverage" as it is called in the trade. REIT's although they have borrowings tend not to be levered to the same extent as they are not expansion oriented. REIT's tend to have their specialties in that you can find a REIT that owns only strip malls, office towers, apartments or hotels. For me, if I were looking at owning one of these "sausages" I'd prefer mine to have a little pork, a little beef and some veal in other words exposure across the entire spectrum of the real estate market. If you have the ability to spot the over stock in the vegetable aisle you certainly can see that if the skyline is littered with cranes building office towers that it might be better to look at hotels or strip malls as a place for your REIT money.

I know, this is worse than planning a dinner party menu. What to have and what not to have. You can see that you are coming down the quality scale. What's left to look at technology? Please spare me. We have already discussed that previously and it does have the smell of old fish about it. Well how about mining? What is a mine? It is a hole in the ground from which the owners are going to extract a known inventory of metal and then close it. That's right, once the inventory is gone the business is finished. How's that for a great business model? But wait a minute the company executives are telling us how they've got this great exploration program that is going to replace the reserves, that is the inventory. Sure they're betting the shareholder's money at 144 to one odds that they are going to find something. I'd rather pull a slot machine handle. No, they insist this is a sure thing. It's a proven mining property in some paragon of democracy, a country in Africa or Latin America. You might be inclined to ask the management of the mining company why there is a proven undeveloped mining asset lying fallow in this country where only a few months ago the locals were being shot dead on the streets by the government. The reason usually is that the mine was nationalized during the previous military junta's term of government. This new government is much more practical and they can see the benefits that will flow to the local economy (and their pockets) should the mine be brought back into production. In most cases that enlightenment lasts until the company invests its capital to bring the mine to production, capital which is immobile, and then the mining laws are changed as the will of the people has to be addressed. The mine is once more an asset of the people, sort of. The conclusion for mining is that the current asset is being depleted and the future asset has a 144 to one chance of being found or lays in a country where ownership is hard to define and the definition fleeting.

It can't be that black and white you say. Yes, you are right, it is not. There is an area of mining that is rare and fruitful. That is the mining of industrial or quasi-industrial minerals under contract. Companies that have long term contracts (20 year plus) to produce commodities like iron ore, limestone, uranium and bauxite for a single source buyer are suitable because the inventory will last beyond your life time and the contract is a willing one between two captive parties. It is much like a marriage, very difficult and messy to get out of and not in the best interest of either party to nullify that contract. There are listed on the exchanges companies that supply commodities such as iron ore to a single buyer with contracts that reflect current market prices and the costs of inflation.

There might be something in the aisle of oil companies. These are like mining companies but wearing long pants. They are a little more mature in that the exploration risk to replace the inventory being sold daily is a lot lower. So low that in eras of new exploration technology, success has led to an excess of supply. That new technology also leads to larger exploration expenditures such that failures can be costly. Dry holes can now cost hundreds of millions of dollars. The easily accessible reserves in politically stable countries have been found so that companies are now exploring in areas with questionable property rights. However, all those risks are built into the share price so that the high dividend yields offered by the major oil companies reflect the full extent of the investor's fears.

The major oil companies make money from producing crude oil and refining it for themselves and others. Their products will always be in demand as the amount of renewable energy is fixed and finite. The amount of solar energy which drives solar panels, wind farms and hydro dams is limited to the amount of sunlight transmitted daily to this planet. That cannot be changed. Whatever shortfall occurs will have to be made up from fossil fuels. That business is here to stay. What to look for? Long life reserves and extensive processing capacity.

For the rest of the cart you are looking at a melange. The easy part has been done and now you are faced with a plethora of businesses. To isolate the ones acceptable to you look for those dividend paying companies that are in a business with difficult levels of entry, protected markets and good margins. They are out there and looking for them is more fun than daytime television.

Common Shares? But They Are So Common

What we have been looking at is common shares. Then why anyone would buy a common share with its inherent risk, you might ask. The reason is that there is the possibility that business growth (as you saw with your nephew's bicycle courier undertaking) will lead to ever increasing earnings. In a perfect world that should lead to increased payouts to the shareholders and this does occur with mature companies controlled by men and women who have gone beyond the need to expose their knees. When I worked at the old Kennecott Mining Company and proposed an exploration program to the board of directors the question that would inevitably come up was, "Will this affect the dividend payout?" I can assure you that there was not a pair of short trousers in the room.

Younger investors seeking growth for their funds will sacrifice the security of the assured semi-annual fixed payment from a bond or debenture in favor of a hoped for increasing stream of payouts from a common share. "Is there no middle ground?" you ask.

There is a less used manner of paying the investors in a company and that is with "preferred" shares. A preferred share (often referred to in the jargon as a "pref") is a share with a fixed price and fixed dividend rate. They are usually issued for a fixed period of time although perpetuals are not uncommon. The banks still issue these as part of their capital base so you see something like a Royal Bank 5 percent, $100 preferred share, callable on December 31, 2050 in the market place. That is a share which has a nominal value of $100 which at the discretion of the board of directors will pay a dividend annually to the extent of $5. The shares were issued at a price of around $100 depending on interest market conditions at the time and will be redeemed by the bank for $100. It is important to note if the shares are required to be redeemed on December 31, 2050 or if the issuer merely has the *right* or *option* to redeem them after that date.

The issue is called preferred because its dividend must be paid before the common shareholders can be paid. In some cases the preferred shares are issued as "cumulative" which means that any unpaid dividends accrue and are an obligation to pay in the future before the common shareholders are paid.

The reason that corporations will issue preferred shares is that they have the option of not paying the dividend. Unlike the other fixed price security, the bond or debenture, there is no liability attached to not paying the preferred share dividend and it is not a bankruptcy causing event. The impetus to pay comes from the restriction on common dividends while the preferred are not paid. Also, if the issue is cumulative any missed dividend will have to be paid in the future adding further impetus to pay.

For the investor (not the trader or speculator) these shares offer an income with tax advantages. Most countries offer some sort of tax relief for dividend income[36], while interest income is taxed

---

36   A corporation will pay income taxes on its earnings. The remainder after tax should be considered tax paid capital or funds belonging to the owners after tax have been paid. It is immoral to double tax people and the concept of taxing dividends is just that, a double taxation. Therefore tax relief is given to dividend recipients.

purely and simply as income with no relief. The market prices of the shares are determined by the current interest scenario. Would you not pay a premium for a previously issued preferred share in the market with a 5 percent yield when current newly issued preferreds are paying only 3 percent? Conversely, why would you sell your 5 percent preferred share for $100 when the new $100 preferred shares are only paying 3 percent? However what you do know is that on the redemption date you will get $100. And there is another benefit of the preferred share over the corporate bond; most preferred share are listed on an exchange with a relatively liquid market. This is not the case for corporate bonds which are traded by over the counter without a clearly posted buy and sell price.

I am sure that you can see that there are significant advantages to this kind of investment. You are assured your payment before the common shareholders (but after the debt holders) and you know how much you will get. As well, instead of having to pay to sell this paper at some point in time it will be redeemed. The drawback is that the dividend is fixed, while with the common shares, the dividend would increase should the company's profits increase.

The Investment that Does Everything

If an acquaintance informed you that there was a new appliance available that laundered your clothes, dried your laundry, washed the dishes and fed the dog you would be highly skeptical. However, I often see otherwise rational investors sidetracked by the investment that will lower or eliminate their taxes and provide superb investment results all in the same piece of paper.

Let's look at taxes first. There are two ways to minimize your tax burden; one is to evade taxes and the other to avoid them. Evading taxes is the process of lying to the tax collector to prevent a false picture of your tax liability. This is a crime. The other option is to avoid taxes by legally adopting structures that operate in your favor to the cost of the tax man. In England in 1936, Lord Merton in a case pitting the UK tax collector (the Inland Revenue Service), against the Duke of Westminster, Lord Merton, hearing the case, ruled that "A man had the right to arrange his financial affairs in a manner so as to attract the minimum amount of tax". Canada was at the time a Dominion of the UK and any constitutional laws passed there applied to the Dominions. So entrenched is the concept of tax avoidance that the US Supreme Court Justice, Oliver Wendell

Homes, upheld it in 1929 in the USA and the first economist, Adam Smith, advocated it.

Many Canadians are unrepentant tax avoiders in that they continuously take advantage of RRSP's, TFSA's and other forms of tax free savings. The few opponents that you hear complaining of tax avoidance are those unable to do so or are beneficiaries of the tax system in the form of government handouts. The question arises as to what else is available beyond the conventional programs mentioned above. The answer is that if it is not government sponsored it is probably illegal. If it does have government backing in some form it is probably legal but unprofitable.

The most common touted investment and tax dodge in Canada is the "flow through share" program. This came about because junior mining exploration caused the expenditure of sums that could never be recouped unless the exploration was successful. As was shown previously the success ratio was 1 in 144, leaving a lot of that exploration expenditure of no benefit to those speculators who had paid for it. If an operating mining company put up the money to explore the "Dead Beat" property and it proved uneconomic the company could charge the exploration expense to its operating income. The question was then asked "If the companies can, why can't individuals?" The Canadian Government looked at this and saw it as a reasonable question. As well, if individuals could charge the natural resources exploration they paid for through speculative share purchases there would be more money flowing into exploration providing employment and the possibility of major new discoveries of minerals. That reasoning was extended to scientific research and other speculative undertakings.

The mechanism was that a speculator/investor bought a special share issue from a resource company that entitled the holder of that share to charge against their income the amount of the value of that shareholding which was expended on exploration. Therefore, if you bought 10,000 shares of Old Gold Exploration's 'flow through' shares at one dollar each for a total of $10,000 and the company was required to spend your $10,000 on exploration then you could deduct the $10,000 from your income. Well you might ask, "What advantage is that to me? I just reduced my taxable income by $10,000 by giving away $10,000 to a mining company. Maybe I should have bought a fur coat."

Firstly, the $10,000 spent on the fur coat would not be accepted by the tax man as a reasonable deduction even if you lived in Nunavut. Secondly, if you had paid a $1.00 for each of your shares and the company made a massive find of gold in Wawa, Ontario your shares would now be worth considerably more than a $1.00 each.

When this program was first introduced I was a neophyte mining analyst and I was curious as to the investment benefits of the idea. I went downstairs to the sales floor and asked my favorite grizzled old stock broker if flow through shares deserved consideration.

"Well, young man if you participate in a flow through share, are you speculating or tax planning?"

"Both," I replied.

"When you work out at the gym, do you play squash and swim at the same time?"

"Of course not, that would be impossible."

"Tax planning and investing are not the same thing. Do one or the other. When you put your money into an RRSP you are tax planning. When you then go on to buy some shares or bonds, you are investing. Note that you don't do the two at the same time."

I thought about his comments and realized that as usual, the old goat was right. I could find better exploration bets than the ones offering flow through shares and I could pursue better tax planning vehicles than the tax driven shares. I then advised clients that if they had an unquenchable desire to participate in the flow through share programs, they should realize that the 1 to 144 odds of mining exploration success would result in their having received shares that would most likely be worthless and a legal tax deduction. If you are going to have nothing material to show at the end of the day, why not give the money to a tax deductible charity?

The program also included oil exploration, but except for wildcat exploration where the results are either a duster, dribbler or gusher, there were fewer flow through issues. The odds of success in oil exploration are considerably better than those of the mining industry. In the oil industry exploration is usually carried out by well-funded large companies with income to offset the exploration costs, hence the minimal need for flow through oil issues.

The accounting for oil and mining exploration is relatively straight forward and the Government was content that the money was being spent properly. However, scientific research is not as simple an accounting regime. When scientific research was presented as just another form of exploration the government acquiesced and scientific research was accorded tax deductibility to the ordinary tax payer. This may have been the start to the abuses that then arose in the tax avoidance schemes that eventually went on to include charitable donations as well as art. It was much more difficult to value the art given to aid charitable work and abuses arose.

In the final instance these investment/tax schemes are like the dishwasher, clothes washer, dryer and dog feeder in one unit. If there were such a device you could be assured after use that the dishes would be spotted, the clothes stained and damp and the dog would die of hunger.

Lady It Looks Like There Is A DRIP In Your Portfolio

I am sure you have had the experience where there is a small trickle coming from under the sink turning into a large invoice coming from a plumber. Although plumbing drips can be a nuisance investment DRIP's are a lady investor's friend.

DRIP's are **D**ividend **R**e-**I**nvestment **P**rograms. Some companies offer you the option of taking your dividend in shares rather than cash. The advantage to you is that you receive treasury shares (often at a slight discount to market) and with no commission. There are a number of advantages to these programs other than the monetary.

If I have convinced you to become a real investor then you will be receiving payment for the use of your money throughout the year. If you are like most serious investors you will have marked in your calendar the day upon which you receive the dividend. This is known as the payment date as opposed to the declaration and ex-dividend dates. You will see in the business press a date upon which the board has declared a dividend is to be paid. That is the date of the formal announcement, sort of like the date you announced your daughter's engagement although the marriage was to take place sometime in the future. The engagement corresponds to the ex-dividend date. On the ex-dividend date anyone who purchases the stock after that date cannot expect to receive the announced dividend. This is analogous to your daughter accepting no more suitors after the engagement date. The payment date is the equivalent of the marriage date. That is when everyone gets their due. Thankfully for dividends there is no divorce equivalent.

Typically a company might announce on May 6th, a dividend payable to shareholders of record June 5th to be paid on June 15th. This means that if you are a shareholder as of close of business on June 5th you will be paid on June 15th. If you were to purchase the shares and be a shareholder of record on June 6th you are out of luck as far as receiving the dividend. This of course affects the share price. Once the dividend is announced there could be a flurry of buying of the shares prior to the ex-dividend date to facilitate receiving the dividend followed by a subsequent falloff in the share price the day after the ex-dividend date. This is tax driven in that the dividend is tax shielded and the capital loss of selling the share after the dividend has been paid can be used to offset capital gains.

For a DRIP participation your purchase price is usually set at 95 percent of the market price over the recent past. If the shares are extremely depressed the corporation cannot renege on the re-investment program and you get your shares[37]. In this way the DRIP program resembles dollar averaging.

Your participation in the DRIP allows you to forego having to calendar the payment date and a decision as to what to do with the dividend. You can usually determine if a company has a DRIP by going on their website and using the search feature.

---

37 There have been instances where companies have concluded that their shares are so downtrodden that the investors are warned in advance of the future cancellation of DRIP programmes. This has occurred with high payout securities such as REITs

Would You Like To Look Under The Hood?

That is the question often asked by car vendors in the hope that the buyer will believe that this is really an exceptional vehicle. We have looked under the hood of the model offered by the investment industry so now I will take you to the corner of the lot where there is an alternative vehicle.

It would be nice to be able to invest without an advisor completely but for older investors the structure of the market place makes it impossible. There is a simple rule of thumb you should be aware of and that is your age should determine the basic structure of your portfolio. The rule states that the percentage of your portfolio invested in fixed income securities (bonds, debentures, preferred shares) should equal your age. Therefore if you are 62 years old your portfolio should hold 62 percent of its value in other than shares. This makes life simple for those of us wearing support hose as the universe of bonds is governed by ratings from AAA (very secure) to CCC (not so secure). The return or earnings from those fixed income securities is directly proportional to their ratings with the highest security bonds (AAA) yielding less than the more risky paper (CCC). Knowing the rating you need not have to "look under the hood" as that has already been done for you and is expressed in the rating.

The highly secure paper is usually not listed on an exchange in Canada. So you can't look up the price of a government, bank or utility bond in the paper. Hopefully, this may change in the future and you will see posted volumes that can be bought or sold and at what prices. These securities are currently traded "over the counter" which means that someone is offering to sell or buy a certain amount at a certain price. This is an actual person. As a result when you want to buy something in that market you have to interface with a real human being. If you were 60 years old and wanted to split your bond portfolio into one third each of AAA, BBB, and CCC bonds the CCCs might be listed on an exchange but the AAA and BBBs would require the services of a broker. Your on line account is only for placing orders. You can't look for securities or advice on line. When you are placing an order electronically or through a service representative[38]it is expected that you have already determined what you want to do and need only execute the trade. Let us assume that you have decided what you want and it is a Bank of Montreal bond maturing in the year 2020. You can't instruct the person at the on line call centre where you invest to find that for you as they are only there to accept instructions to trade. You have to use the services of an advisor. You need a conventional account.

To begin, if you announce that the account you are opening with the broker will deal only in bonds (as you intend to use the on line account for equities) he may politely decline to accept the account. His reason is that even if yours is a $5 million account it is worthless to him. Over the counter markets for unlisted securities such as bonds are based on a spread. That means that the trader or person providing that Bank of Montreal 2020 bond is offering to

---

38   Most on line services will charge a premium if you have to place an order through a representative as they expect you to deal electronically through your computer screen.

sell it at $1005 per bond and buy it at $999 per bond. **There is no commission; the profit accrues directly to the trader from the difference in prices.** If your broker bought you a million dollars of the Bank of Montreal bonds he would make not a dime. If he bought you a million dollars of Bank of Montreal common shares he would make about $5,000 because he need only place the order for that listed security and charge his commission.

For the broker's firm the bond account is more than worthless, it is a loss leader. The firm has to maintain the account, provide reports and collect the interest. When the million dollar bond transaction was executed the trader on the firm's bond desk will have booked a profit but that does not show up in the accounts of the equity sales manager. To make it worse if you bought that 2020 bond in 2012 there would not be the occasion for another million dollar trade for eight years when the bond matures and is redeemed.

Some years ago I introduced a broker to the money making ways for his clients by investing in (but not trading) bonds. He was a clever chap and recognized the merits of the method and began following my philosophy and his client base grew as did their fortunes. He became so adept that he took the philosophy to the condominium market. Condominiums have reserve funds to provide for future repair expenses and these are invested in AAA or AA bonds. My acolyte had captured a third of the downtown condominium reserve fund market and was increasing that. His firm fired him. His commission sheets did not show the minimum required for employment with the august bank owned brokerage although his book of business was one of the largest at the firm.

You may find a bank broker willing to take your bond only account but his firm is expecting a quid pro quo. That usually is in the expectation of cross selling such products as mortgages, credit cards, bank loans or insurance. Therefore your first choice of potential help should be at the bank where you are currently banking.

The process of opening an advisor account involves the "Know Your Client" form or KYC as it is known in the trade. On this form the broker will want to record your level of risk tolerance and knowledge of financial markets. His best choices are 100 percent risk tolerance and complete understanding of financial markets. In that way he can recommend anything from speculative mining stocks to government bonds. Your best position is zero market sophistication and minimal tolerance for risk. Your new found broker's hands are tied even if only with dental floss.

Remember that the only reason you are using this traditional broker is that he can provide you access to the government and corporate bond markets. If in the future there should be a listed market for these securities then you could move your traditional bond account to your on line account. In the interim you would expect this broker to provide you with recommendations in which to invest. He need do no research as you are buying the range of BBB to AAA rated bonds. Seeing as they are rated by a bond rating agency which has examined the safety of the issue, there is no need for him to examine the outlook for the issuer. His input to the investment analysis and decision is minimal and you should expect to pay him nothing and at worst a token amount.

The Wind Through Your Hair

Remember when you were young and someone in the crowd had a convertible. There was an exhilarating feeling of riding down the road in an open top car. You may also remember that your father would comment on the hazards of a car with no roof and quote you statistics from the insurance companies as to the fatalities and accidents accruing to open cars being much higher than conventional sedans. The insurance companies demanded a higher premium to compensate for that risk.

Yes, convertibles are riskier, not only vehicles, but bonds as well. There is available in the market place a convertible bond or debenture. This is a bond which provides the holder the privilege of going to the company treasury and demanding shares in exchange for his bond. Supposing Mammoth Industries has issued $100 million dollars' worth of convertible debentures (convertible at the rate of 100 shares per debenture). How does that differ from a conventional bond and how is it similar?

The similarities are that:

- Each bond has a $1,000 par or fixed value, the value prescribed by the issuer and the amount to be received at redemption date,
- The interest or coupon rate is fixed, (let's say 5 percent),
- The redemption date is fixed (let's say December 30, 5 years out, as of this writing 2022)

The differences are:

- Each bond is convertible into the company shares at a fixed rate, in this case (100 shares per bond certificate of $1,000 par)

If you were to purchase one bond certificate at par ($1,000) and immediately demand your 100 shares from the company it would be the equivalent of paying $1,000 for 100 shares or $10.00 per share (purchase price $1,000/ 100 shares). In the same way a bond convertible into 200 shares would, bought at par and converted immediately gives you a purchase price $5.00 per share ($1,000 purchase price /200 shares). It is important to note that you are under no obligation to convert your bond or debenture into common shares, and that you have been provided that privilege at your option.

For many corporations the conversion of the debentures to shares is preferred to redeeming at par. Therefore if the debentures are trading at a premium as a result of the conversion[39] and thus to the debenture holders benefit, the company may call the paper for redemption. The debenture holder seeing his security quoted at $1,200 because the underlying shares are worth $1,200 will choose to exercise the conversion rather than present the bond for redemption at $1,000. This is often referred to as a "forced conversion".

For a bond or debenture all the specifications remain fixed (redemption date, par value, coupon – interest rate, and for a convertible the number of shares received in exchange for the bond).

---

39   This is described in investment parlance as "being in the money".

The price at which the bond or debenture trades in the market place is not fixed. The market can ascribe a value of $700, $2,200 or whatever it pleases to a $1,000 par debenture. That does not alter any of the parameters we have fixed and listed above. If you purchased one of Mammoth Industries 5 percent convertible debentures of December 30, 2022, you have effectively lent the company $1,000 until December 30th, 2017 and you expect to get paid $50.00 per year for that loan. That is written in stone.

Current practice says that seeing as there is an equity or share component to the Mammoth debenture (the convertible into shares feature) it should be listed on an exchange. You now have the situation that a security with an ascribed value ($1,000) is going to be traded on the exchange for 5 years. What price should it trade at?

Ignoring the convertible feature, if Mammoth Industries was a company with only $100 million in debt costing $5 million a year in interest cost while its operations produced cash flow of $50 million a year and its assets were worth $1.5 billion, the paper would certainly trade at par. The reasons being that an investor would look at the $50 million annual cash flow and reckon that the company was earning enough to cover the bonds interest cost ten times over. As well, in the case of bankruptcy the assets of the firm at $1.5 billion cover the debt outstanding by a factor of 15 times. With only 5 years of term the paper would, in normal times, trade at par or a premium.

The convertible feature can change the market price of Mammoth's debenture irrespective of its pure bond fundamentals. Looking at the share price at the time of the issue of the Mammoth 5 percents of 2022 it was trading at $9.00 per share. So if on the date of issue you had purchased a debenture and immediately exercised the conversion feature your cost would have been as shown above be $10 per share for 100 shares trading in the free market at $9.00. If you now tried to sell the shares just acquired you would only receive $900. It would be economically foolish to exercise your conversion privilege because you can sell the bond in the market place at par ($1,000) or convert it and sell the shares received for only $900. Obviously, you won't exercise your conversion privilege and continue to view your investment as an interest paying security.

What would the situation look like if sometime later the shares of Mammoth Industries are trading on the exchange at $15.00 each? You pull out your certificate and see that it is exchangeable for 100 shares. There is no mention of price, just the 100 shares. You quickly calculate that 100 shares multiplied by the current share price are worth $1,500. What would you do? You would immediately slip the bond certificate into a FedEx envelope and send it to Mammoth Industries' transfer agent and demand that it be exchanged for 100 shares that should be sent to you. A week later the shares arrive and you sell them pocketing $1,500, returning a profit to you of $500 for a certificate you only paid $1,000 for.

Thrilled by your success you go on line or call your broker to buy more of the Mammoth Industries 5% convertible debentures of 2022 at $1,000 each, but alas they are no longer trading at $1,000 they are on offer at $1,500. The reason being that every other participant in the market place knows that if they were to purchase a $1,000 debenture for $1,500 they could immediately liquidate it for $1,500 by exercising the conversion privilege (the efficient market thesis again in operation). Therefore no one is going to offer a $1,000 par Mammoth Industries debenture for less than $1,500. In fact rather than converting your debenture to shares and then selling the shares to obtain your $1,500 and $500 profit you could have just as easily sold your debenture on the exchange for $1,500.

As well it is not necessary for you to deliver the bond to the transfer agent, you can have your on line account facilitate that transaction.

I can hear your mind spinning. This is far more exciting than the wind in the hair routine. This offers some security as well as potential protection from the nemesis of the bond market, inflation.

The threat that bond investor's endure is that the purchasing power they receive at redemption will be less than that at the time of the bond's purchase the convertible bond offers protection from that as the underlying value of the shares, in many cases, will reflect the ravages of inflation. Let's talk about inflation.

The Fifth Horseman
Of The Apocalypse

There is no greater wealth killer than inflation. Inflation is the creation of money in excess of the rate of growth of the economy. Let's say you live in an economy where there are 100 assets and 100 one dollar bills in circulation. Each asset would have a cash value of one dollar:

---

100 dollars/ 100 assets   =   1 dollar/ asset

Now let's assume that the government decides to print another 100 dollars so that the amount in circulation is now 200 dollars. What is an asset worth?

---

200 dollars/ 100 assets   = 2 dollars / asset

If you lived in that society and woke up one morning after inflation had occurred you might have gone to the marketplace with your dollar in hand expecting to buy one asset unaware that inflation had occurred overnight. The asset vendor would inform you that you were too late as assets now cost 2 dollars each. I know, this sounds like fraud. However as always a practice that has been in place for a prolonged period becomes accepted. The first reported use of this fraud to steal the citizenry's purchasing power was by the playwright Euripides around 420 B.C. in his play "The Frogs".

> Where is the silver drachma of old?
>
> And the recent gold coins,
>
> So clear stamped and worth their weight,
>
> Through the known world they've ceased to circulate,
>
> Now Athenian shoppers go to market with their pockets full of shoddy silver plated coppers.

This was written during the Peloponnesian War. Wars are costly undertakings, at the end of which you have very little to show for your expenditures. The Athenians had difficulty continuing to pay for their war so they took to debasing their currency. This was done by taking the coins in circulation which were solid silver and re-melting them to add 50 percent copper. They now had twice as many coins in circulation and so could once more meet their fiscal obligations. As you saw from Euripides comment this eventually lead to the coins being solid copper coated with silver.

Let's put that into a modern context. Do you remember the US Roosevelt dime? It was a ten cent piece and until 1971 contained, as many US coins did, an amount of silver based on an ounce of silver being worth $1.25. That meant that a silver dollar contained 0.80 ounces of silver ($1.00/$1.25 = 0.80). So a dime or one tenth of a dollar would contain a tenth of the amount of silver as that of a silver dollar or .08 ounces of silver. If you found one of those pre-1971 dimes in your pocket it would be worth $2.80 with the silver price, at this writing, of $30 per ounce (.08 X $30 = $2.40). That implies that price levels have increased 24 times ($2.40/$.10

= 24). Yes that's right. A house you could have bought in 1970 for $30,000 now sells for $720,000.

If you were to take the approach of creating currency to ease your fiscal woes you would find yourself in jail charged with what is called counterfeiting. If a government eases its budgetary discomfort by printing more money it's called monetary policy. No matter who does it, increasing the money supply beyond the rate of growth of the economy leads to inflation. This is the situation where there is a general increase in the nominal prices of all products without any increase in their intrinsic value. The beneficiaries of this are those in debt who are now paying their creditors with less purchasing power than they borrowed. The largest debtor in any society is the government. It is extremely convenient for them that they have control of the national currency printing press as they can put it to good use.

The concept of currency debasement is well known in the financial community and they take steps to protect themselves. The lenders when seeing the inflation horseman riding over the horizon even without pestilence, war, famine and disease, react by raising interest rates. Lenders expect to make about 3.5 to 4.5 percent rent or interest on their loans to reasonably secure borrowers. If inflation rates are running at 10 percent per year the actual return to the lender with money on loan at 4 percent is minus 6 percent as there is a 6 percent loss of purchasing power. The rational lender will not lend his money until he gets his four percent net of inflation and the only way he can do that is to charge fourteen percent (4 percent interest + 10 percent inflation). During a lender's strike they place their funds in other than the bonds on offer. They invest in precious metals, oil, real estate or any other hard asset that cannot be replicated or created. They will, as well, purchase the bonds of foreign government borrowers who are not inflating their currency. The lenders always win the strike because the government is a money junkie and the lenders are its dope dealers.

The most obvious sign of impending inflation is the price of gold. Governments cannot print gold. Of the gold in circulation in Julius Caesar's times, 90 percent is still available. Only ten percent of the metal has been lost while at the same time tremendous amounts have been mined in the New World. Interestingly, the vast amounts of precious metals imported to Europe during the 1700's caused a bout of inflation as precious metal coinage was the medium of exchange and here new amounts were being "printed".

Either simultaneously or sequentially you will see inflation in the price of houses and commercial real estate. Buildings are deteriorating assets, just look at the Parthenon in Athens. The wood work rots, the roof deteriorates the floors wear, etcetera, so how can a house that is ten years old be worth more than when it was built? It is the real estate underneath it you will be told. The lot on which the house stands is worth more money. Has the utility of the lot changed: no. It still is the depository of the same old house. What has really happened is the value of the money to buy it has fallen.

Should inflationary times arise, your neighbor, Nick Notsosmart might at some point confide to you over the backyard fence that you are both millionaires as a house similar to yours, down the street has recently sold for a million dollars. Admittedly you only paid $500,000 for the 2,500 square feet in which you are living and so there is an apparent profit. The reality is that if you sold and then wanted to replace your 2,500 square feet house you would end up having to pay a million dollars. The only way you can profit from the increase in real estate prices brought on by inflation is to sell and move into a homeless shelter, unless you were thoughtful enough to purchase two houses one for dwelling and one for speculation. Alas, there is the word we should all hate, speculation. To have bought the extra house would mean that you have "looked into the future and spied out" the events that were to occur. Out of necessity the government has turned you into a speculator as you are betting on asset prices increasing as a result of the falling value of the currency. If you bought the house to earn income, through its rental stream, you are an investor. If you bought the house because of an expected price increase you are a speculator. Mr. Carville, Bill Clinton's campaign manager, was correct; the bond market can intimidate everybody, even you by turning a sensible investor into a betting speculator. If you saw bond prices falling and hence interest returns rising you would react by assuming forthcoming inflation and act accordingly.

What about your portfolio? It contains bank and financial shares. Looking at the financial companies' business plan we see that they borrow for the short term and lend for the long. With interest rates increasing for short term loans and noting that the depositors can redeem their loans immediately by withdrawing their money from the bank, the banks will see an increase in their borrowing costs as they must pay higher interest to maintain their deposits. On the other side of their ledger the loans that they have made are "locked in" for a fixed period. They cannot go to the mortgage borrower or car loan customer with a fixed contract and unilaterally raise the interest rate. The financial companies are the antithesis of the governments in that they are lenders, not borrowers and as such inflation destroys their assets and increases their costs.

We have concluded that the financial shares are going to suffer from an earnings point of view as the high cost of the money they have to borrow in the short term is used to finance the low yielding loans they made in the past. What about the utilities shares you own? They will suffer as well. The pipeline company will charge against its taxes an amount called depreciation to reflect the ageing of its facilities and the cost the company will incur to replace them. The basis of this charge is the historical cost of the asset. As an example let's look at the following income and tax statement for "Hypothetical Pipelines Inc." with a pipeline that cost $100 million to build which is expected to last for 50 years. That means that every year the company must put aside $2 million for 50 years so as to have the funds necessary to replace the asset. The government therefore allows the company to deduct from its income $2 million per year as a "depreciation" charge to build up its coffers. At the end of 50 years it will have enough money to replace the pipeline. In an inflationary environment the price of steel, machinery and labor will all increase and the cost of replacing the pipeline will increase as well. The $100 million saved to build a new service will not be sufficient.

Industrial companies and utilities with large capital investments in inflationary times will not be able to finance their survival from their own earnings. Either dividends will have to be decreased or eliminated or dilutive financings undertaken.

The Silver Bullet

In the pulp novels of the 1930's Dracula and his kind of supernatural monsters were killed with a silver bullet. There is a silver bullet for inflation but is more protective from, than fatal to the monster.

Precious metals can be mined but not created. The "low hanging fruit" in the form or easily found and exploitable deposits have been found and mined. New finds are few and far between, located in dangerous places. Gold, silver and platinum are obvious yard sticks of value that cannot be changed. Yes the price of gold will change but its value, the price of one week's of a labourer's output, will remain constant. So powerful a hedge against inflation are these precious metals that governments such as the United States at times have forbidden their citizens from owning them. What can a government gain by inflating away their debts if the citizens are completely hedged against such depreciation of the currency by holding gold?

During a national period of inflation, if the citizens are allowed to exchange their falling currency for stable gold bars what has been gained? The national currency will fall in comparison to its trading partners as the citizens in the inflating country exchange their paper money for real money, precious metals.

Let's suppose that the government has restricted precious metals ownership, have you any other access to the inflation hedge? Yes, precious metals company shares. A company that owns millions of ounces of precious metal in the ground will see the value of that inventory rise as the posted prices for the metals increases. Don't expect to see marked increases in the company's earnings as they will be subject to the same inflationary forces that everyone else is. However the inventory is worth more and the life span of the mines increased thus revaluing the company and its shares.

Gold has been a problem for traditional old school economists who have branded it as "barbaric", "antiquated" and a "relic" as an investment. Remember that these are people who believe in economies functioning in a classical manner in that inflation will be useful as a deodorant for government financial malodour and thus necessary.

Mark Twain once remarked "Buy real estate. They aren't making any more of it". He was of course correct. So, if like gold the availability of real estate is limited it should then be a "silver bullet" as well and it is. During inflationary periods real estate investment trusts (REIT's) see their prices increase as investors pursue them to hedge against the falling currency. The problem is that REIT's like gold mines will not see their profits or balance sheet valuations of their assets increase immediately but will have to wait for tenant turnover with increasing rents and property sales transactions ascribing higher prices to new properties. The astute investor knows that a property bought last year with inflation at one percent is now worth more with inflation running at 10 percent.

The problem with inflation is that is often hidden. There isn't much use in trying to defraud your currency holders if they know its value is going to be compromised. Therefore you will often see inflation rates posted by government which include a basket of consumer commodities but exclude gasoline and food. Perhaps you know of group of consumers that don't drive or eat. Please don't bring up the Amish, as although they don't drive, they do eat.

There is as well a tendency in government to attempt to place the blame on inflation on the effects it causes. You will see in the press that inflation is rising because of wage pressure. Actually wage demands are being fuelled by reduced purchasing power stemming from increased inflation. You will in your investing career see many similar attributions to rising inflation whereas the world's most eminent economists have described it as a purely monetary phenomenon. That phenomenon is an increase in the money supply.

The Sixth Horseman or
Your Silent Partner

Like all income, investment income attracts tax, interest and dividends when received and capital gains when taken. At the outset you can see that your capital gains taxation is at your discretion. When you sell the asset is when you will attract tax. Obviously that leads to tax planning capabilities, also known as tax avoidance.

For example if you had a gain in a share or bond holding in your accounts and the year end was approaching your best strategy would be to wait until the new year to take your gain by selling the security as it would be taxable in your latest taxation year which has just started. You will therefore put off paying tax on your gain for the better part of a year. Also if you had capital losses you might choose to sell your loosing investments at year end and then sell some of your winning ones so that your net capital loss versus gain was zero. You would offset your losses with gains and as such take advantage of the losses you have occurred to offset your gains. Starting in late November you will see trading coming into the market when this phenomenon takes place as investors capture both their losses and gains to bring about a flat position for the current taxation period.

In Canada, capital gains first started attracting tax in 1972 as a result of the philosophy of the then Finance Minister, Edgar Benson, which was, "a buck is a buck". This was interpreted that it did not matter how you earned the "buck", it was all the same and subject to tax. At first capital losses could be charged against either earned or investment income in keeping with that spirit. The realization was not long in coming that the majority of taxpayers were not investors but speculators who consistently lost money and were now able to charge that against other sources of income lowering Ottawa's total take. The tax act was changed to only allow the charging of capital losses against capital gains, however to provide a degree of fairness, losses could be offset by gains the taxpayer may have had in the previous five years and carried forward into the future. In that way a taxpayer incurring a loss in this year could offset it against his past five years of gains and if that were not enough he could hope to make sufficient gains in the next few years to absorb his remnant losses.

The other fairness aspect was the level of taxation on capital gains. The government realized that speculating and investing were fraught with risk, therefore, to tax speculative income the same as safe earnings income would be inherently unfair. The Canadian government's approach was to tax only half of the capital gain incurred. Therefore, if you bought a security for $100 and sold it for $200 you would have a $100 capital gain of which only half, or $50, would be taxable. That $50 is added to your income and taxed at your highest marginal rate. If you were in a 40 percent tax bracket for your last earned dollar, your tax cost of the $100 capital gain would be 40 percent charged on half the gain or 40 percent of $50 which would mean you would send a cheque to Ottawa for $20. You in effect paid a 20 percent tax rate, the lowest you will pay on any kind of income. This low rate of taxation has the perverse effect of causing otherwise rational people to try to maximize their capital gains income to achieve a low tax rate. As one grouchy old broker asked his client, "Are you investing to earn money or save taxes?"

Next on the money making schemes for the tax man is dividend income. When you file your tax form you will notice that your dividend income is subject to all sorts of machinations the end result being you are given a tax reduction on the original amount. This dividend tax credit is to compensate for the fact that the money earned by your corporation is taxed and the dividend is an after tax payment. Logically, it should not be taxed at all and considered a return of capital and hence not income and not subject to tax. That, however, would be too costly for the tax man. If you were to receive $1.00 in dividends, the tax credit would bring that down to an effective payment to you of about $0.70, the amount on which you would pay tax. To the investor, $1.00 of dividends is, on an after tax basis, more valuable than $1.00 in interest payments. For the taxpayer a dollar of interest is taxed at her full marginal rate and assuming the 40 percent tax rate results in her receiving only $0.60 after tax. The $1.00 dividend having been reduced to $0.70 for tax purposes will attract $0.28 of tax at a 40 percent rate. Taking the original dividend as having been paid at and received by you as $1.00 your net profit after tax is $0.72 compared to the $0.60 received after tax from the $1.00 of interest earned.

The financial markets being efficient, are aware of the difference in tax treatment and therefore adjust the price of securities to reflect this. If interest rates were currently six percent, the security providing the $0.60 in after tax interest would be priced at $10.00 to yield you six percent before tax (6% X $10 = $.60). To be equivalent to an after tax interest yield of six percent, the dividend paying security would have to be priced at $12.00 (6% X $12 = $.72). This is exactly what you see in security markets. What appears to be the same amount of pre-tax income, one dollar, from a security which pays it in the form of dividends is priced higher than the equivalent interest paying security because of the tax treatment accord the different payment forms. This also leads to another investment strategy. People with high income tax rates will often choose to take dividend income rather than interest income and vice versa in that people with low or zero income tax rates will choose interest over dividends. This then begs the question, "How can my tax rate be zero?" That situation arises when your investment funds are in a "registered" investment pool such as a Tax Free Saving Account (TFSA) or Registered Retirement Savings Plan (RRSP). In that case obviously your best strategy is to choose interest over dividends. Yes, your RRSP pays zero tax until you take it out. Your TFSA is completely tax free.

Obviously the benign tax regime for capital gains or dividends has no functionality in a tax free account. If you accept the higher risk investment such as speculation or dividends in a tax shielded account you will achieve no after tax reward commensurate with having taken the risk. Remember that dividends can be eliminated by the payer and most speculations are failures.

The Government encouraged savings plans such as retirement, education and long term savings accounts by having their income shielded from taxation. In this way the government can encourage the programs without having to put up money, but just forego income. When these plans are unwound they attract tax (except for the TFSA) but in the interim, they earn without tax. For retirement programs this ensures a debate as to whether to own dividend paying shares or interest paying bonds. Both camps are right.

For those who have just suffered through the horrors of adolescence and are now becoming rational human beings, the dividend earning retirement plan makes some sense. Okay, I know there are few post-adolescents who have yet acquitted themselves of their concepts of immortality and immediate gratification and not started saving for retirement, but let's assume that such a person exists. If one of your children or grandchildren can be induced into thinking of the concept of retirement they will be looking at 40 years of pension savings. If, in the first half of that period, there occurs a few years without dividend increases or a missed dividend or two this will not lead to food bank style retirement. As well, if the young adult's investments are in companies with growing dividend streams, the share prices will increase to maintain the yields at constant levels. When the plan is cashed out at retirement there will be no distinction as to how the plan earned its income, it will all be taxed as pure income with no consideration for the capital gains or dividend portions. Therefore, the only reason to own the dividend paying shares is if they have dividend growth. The types of shares that have that potential are first the financial companies' shares and secondly the utilities. When your youngster comes around asking about how you managed to retire in dignity point out that in your youth you owned a portfolio of dividend paying shares without consideration of their price growth and used the DRIP programs to continue to increase your holdings. Note, I said in your youth.

If you are 25 years old and you lose five percent of your retirement savings to a bad investment you have 35 years to regain it. The device which so intrigued Einstein that he called the eighth wonder of the world, was compound interest. It will recover that for you within a decade. If you lose that same five percent when you are 65 years old it will be a larger amount because your savings should be greater at 65, and you may not have a decade to recover it. I mentioned previously that a portfolio should be weighted on the basis of your age. If you are 65 years old then 65 percent of your portfolio should be in fixed income or similar highly secure investments. "No Hope Silver Corp of Nevada" does not meet that criterion.

In the final instance, for the untaxed account the best investment is an interest bearing instrument. The reasons being that the payments from the investment are mandatory and the principal to some degree secured. The magic of compound interest will take care of the growth.

In some jurisdictions such as Canada, investors are required to begin collapsing their tax shielded registered accounts after a certain age. This means that you will withdraw at least a minimum amount from the shielded account and pay taxes on that as if it were earned income. What to do with the balance? Invest it in a garden variety account either on line or with a broker. If you go on line then the easiest approach is to find some exchange traded funds (ETF) to meet your needs. These would likely be dividend and bond funds. These will provide you with an income with minimal costs because you will seldom if ever trade them and the management fees are usually less than 0.05 percent.

The End Game

If you observed all the warnings I gave you and kept your stock broker on a tight leash you probably have a nice nest egg now that you are turning 71. I realize that your hair dresser says you appear to be 55, but the fact is the tax man in Canada is well aware of your age and after 71 you are no longer allowed to contribute to your Registered Retirement Savings Plan (RRSP) and you are in fact required to start taking out money. You may ask, why is it necessary to start withdrawing? As you know your money in the RRSP is earning tax free income and the Government believes that after age 71 it is entitled to tax some of that. Therefore, after 71 you are required to start winding down your (RRSP) by converting it to a Registered Retirement Investment Fund (RRIF) or an annuity. The difference between a RRIF and an RRSP is that with the RRIF you are required to take possession in your hands of a portion of the fund, starting at 7 percent annually[40]. If you had built up an RRSP of $1 million and converted it to a RRIF you would be required in the subsequent year to take $70,000 (7% X $1million = $70,000) out of the fund and pay tax on it. Assuming you can continue to generate five percent within the fund you should be able to stretch

---

40   The rates being quoted are nominal as they are politically sensitive and hence subject to change.

your payment out for between 20 and 25 years. Somewhere between 91 and 96 years of age you will have eroded away your entire fund.

You will find as you age that your spending patterns will change gradually. Being in that yummy Italian Restaurant will be grand but getting there is an annoyance. What were once highly anticipated pleasures now begin to be inconveniences. As a result although you are required to withdraw funds from the RRIF you may not be spending it all. The home for those funds will be an investment account which will be biased towards the bond market.

Another option is the annuity. An annuity is a contract between, usually an insurance company and a beneficiary, to receive a fixed amount of money over a fixed period or the life of the beneficiary. The payment consists of two portions, capital and interest. In early years, seeing as the capital provided is at its peak there is a large interest component on those funds. There is a tax cost associated which is at its peak and declines over time although the payments remain constant.

The most common is a life annuity. In this instance, the pensioner purchases an annuity that will pay her a fixed amount monthly until death. At the time of this writing, a woman aged 71 could buy payments of about $500 per month for life per $100,000 placed with the insurer. Therefore, for a million dollars of after tax funds you could expect $60,000 per year. Any amount that went into the purchase of the annuity that was from savings or other form of capital is not taxable, only the interest earned on that is taxable. Other forms such as untaxed RRSP funds used to purchase an annuity are taxed much more severely because at the time the funds are rolled out of the RRIF or RRSP into the annuity tax is charged at your top rate to give an after tax amount going into the annuity. Therefore if you had a million dollar RRSP you could expect somewhere around $600,000 to be available for the annuity.

Virtually all annuities sold in Canada today come with a guarantee period with ten years being the most common. That means if you die before ten years you can have the balance of the funds transferred to an heir. Most commonly you'll see that the balance is destined for a spouse. Also an annuity can be structured such that a surviving spouse is the beneficiary if the original annuitant should die. The annoying aspect of the life annuity is that if you purchase the annuity today and both you and your spouse die tomorrow and you have no guarantee the funds are lost because they remain with the annuity provider who no longer has to pay you. There are a number of ways to guard against this outcome and most of them involve a life insurance policy in parallel with the annuity and of course the guarantee period.

On the positive side, if your family had a number of members with long life expectancy, then your gene pool could lead to your outliving your expected actuarial demise. Irrespective of this unfortunate outcome for the annuity provider, they still have to pay.

Another option available is the time limited annuity. This instrument provides payments for a fixed period. The amount you receive is prescribed by the amount you purchase and for how long. If you were to purchase a 20 year annuity and die after 5 years, the unused portion of the annuity would become part of your estate and go to your heirs if properly structured. The people who choose these rationalize their decision usually on the concept that as they get older their need for funds decreases. When the 20 year annuity is in its 18th year the recipient (or more correctly annuitant) of the funds would probably have a very low level of spending. You don't see many smartly dressed wheel chair bound octogenarians on cruise ships.

The reasons supporting an annuity as the last stage of investment are because annuities are supplied by insurance companies around the world, the market is highly competitive and the instruments reasonably secure. You could choose to have your annuity with a UK or Swiss provider paying in Canadian dollars if they offered the best returns. This would apply to other than RRSP or RRIF funds which receive some benefits if rolled into a Canadian based annuity.

Seeing as this is a contract between you and the vendor it is difficult to attack in the courts. Although under some circumstances your RRSP or RRIF could be subject to loss to a creditor the annuity in most cases is secure. The security you have to worry about is the creditworthiness of the vendor. Intuitively you would expect that a Canadian insurance company would be a safe supplier with little expectation of bankruptcy, however, remember that not too many years ago the Confederation Life Insurance Company went bankrupt. Although there is some protection for the annuitant in these circumstances there can never be a complete guarantee.

There is another use of annuities that may be of interest. Suppose you have a nephew who is thoroughly convinced that he is the next Keith Richards of Rolling Stone fame. He spends his days abusing a guitar and doing little else. If at your demise you were to leave this aspiring performer a piece of your estate, it is unlikely that it would last for any reasonable period. In situations such as this leaving the person an annuity is the best way to ensure some financial security when you are no longer available to make the handouts.

The annuity provider takes the funds you give them and invests those in the most secure of assets. These being very low risk have very low rates of return. The combination of low returns and oper-ating costs provides you a small payout. As I mentioned at the time of this writing a 71 year old woman could expect to receive about $6,000 per year per $100,000 of annuity purchased would imply an imbedded rate of less than six percent. An investor might do better in a corporate bond portfolio but the investor's return is not guaranteed while the annuitant receives her guaranteed payments irrespective of the state of markets.

When you strip away all the packaging and look at the product on its own merits what you see is guaranteed payments, but what are you giving up? You have no control over your portfolio which is probably a good outcome. As we age the ability to make good strategic decisions fades. You are guaranteed an income, another good thing. The bad part of the bargain is that the "Fifth Horseman of the Apocalypse", inflation, is always waiting in the wings to erode the value of your assets and hence purchasing power. Financial assets are particularly vulnerable, and so overtime you will see the purchasing power of your guaranteed income diminish. The politicians and bureaucrats are aware of this threat (because they created it) and therefore they always have inflation protection attached to their pensions in the form of indexation to the inflation level. This protection is not normally available for the ordinary pensioner.

In the final instance, it is up to you to make the decisions based on what you believe your life expectancy will be. If you have a family history of longevity, the annuity provider must still provide you the same outcome as the average female of your age at the time of purchase. Therefore, a 71 year old woman would pay the same amount for a life annuity as any of her contemporaries irrespective of her family genetics. If you have a history of longevity in your family then the life time annuity is the proper choice. If your parents and siblings die early then a fixed term with an estate payout at death is the answer.

When the time comes to annuitize, and it must be before 85 years of age, contact a number of insurance companies and compare their offerings. You will be talking to an agent, and like everybody in the financial business they will expect to be paid. For a half million dollar or higher annuity, the agent might be willing to shave her commission to land the sale, you therefore have room to negotiate. But what to do if you don't want to annuitize?

The Monster that Ate my Stock Broker

There is no stopping the monster. First it ate the book stores, then the retailers and now the investment industry is being devoured by the beast. The beast of course is the internet.

The investment markets were a natural for the internet to take over as the product (shares) are traded electronically and all that was needed to facilitate the business was an interface between the electronic share trade and the investor's computer and the entrepreneurs were quick to provide that. The stock broker became redundant except that he could provide advice. Seeing as the market is efficient, it is unlikely that the advice provided will ensure portfolio performance better than the market average. This is why mutual funds were invented. As mentioned previously investments in mutual fund companies shares were a sure source of wealth – much better than investments in their funds. However, the monster has eaten the mutual funds as well.

The lowered cost of trading the shares which go into a mutual fund combined with the ability to buy or sell a fund on the exchange has led to the "Exchange Traded Fund" or ETF, as mentioned previously. Unlike their pre-internet brothers they have a minimal administration cost of anywhere as low as 0.5 percent and can be bought with minimal commission of as little as $10.00 to trade any dollar amount you may want to transact. With the mutual fund model the company building the portfolio offers the investors the right to buy and to sell to the sponsor, not the market. Therefore at the end of the day the mutual company determines what the cumulative value of all the shares in the portfolio is worth and posts that for the investors to buy or sell. Computing power has now given a fund administrator the ability to price the fund at the current market of the contained shares and then be able to offer to buy or sell on the exchange the fund at its current real value. To accommodate the speculators, the E.T.F. crowd has constructed funds that match or mirror most highly traded entities such as gold, oil, financial and any other item you may want to bet on. I am not using the word "bet" loosely as that is what these E.T.F.'s are used for. However if you are an investor you can buy an E.T.F. that will provide you dividend income, an exposure to financial companies shares or bonds. Financial commentators have opined that there could in some future time be more ETF's than stocks listed on the exchange. This could arise as the ETF's become more focused. At the time of this writing the number of ETF's showing up in the new high/low listing of the financial press equals the number of shares mentioned.

If you read the book I mentioned, "A Random Walk Down Wall Street" by Burton Malkiel and concluded as I have that no one can beat the market consistently then you will accept the buy and hold thesis. But what to buy? Buy the market.

You can buy E.T.F's that will perfectly reflect the stock market. If you set up your RRSP or RIF in an online account and purchase stock market based ETF's, your investing days are over and you can get on to something more palatable. As money goes into the RRSP from payouts you just re-invest and when it comes time to wind it down you just reduce positions.

While in your active investing years take advantage of any form of DRIP and certainly the "dollar averaging" program which is to invest money at the time you receive it. In this way you will buy irrespective of the market sentiments.

Remember that if your phone, electricity or telecommunications utility, not to mention bank, is gouging you silly with excessive fees, don't complain, buy their shares. They'll be able to pay you a big fat dividend.

Don't forget your Tax Free Savings Account and other tax shelters in to which you can put your money. Remember that at the time of this writing the top marginal rate tax payer will pay:

- 50 percent on Interest income,
- 34 percent on dividend income,
- 25 percent on capital gains.

Obviously the greatest beneficiary of tax shielding is the interest income. Why would you even want to shield capital gains?

What if you don't want to buy an ETF? Are you willing to sit at your computer and search for:

1. Companies that have had a long term dividend history?
2. Companies that have had consistent dividend growth?
3. Companies that trade at a modest price-earnings ratio?
4. Companies that have a long term business model?
5. Companies whose markets are in some way protected?

As you can see it is a daunting task which is why advisors exist. Note that above I did not mention shares or stocks. You are not going to invest in a share as that is impossible. You are going to invest in companies. People who buy shares are speculators intent on selling them at a higher price, maybe. So how can you invest in companies through an advisor and minimize your costs?

The closest you can come is through a fee arrangement. You hire someone to work for you for a fee, let's call her a portfolio manager. Note that means the person cannot work for the broker, she must work for you. You would pay this person an annual fee based on no more than one percent of the value of your portfolio at year end. The only way the portfolio manager can increase her income is if the value of your portfolio increases. Your portfolio manager will be forced by the structure to attempt to minimize fees and costs while maximizing returns. The surest way to do that is to build a portfolio of income producing securities. The worst course for your portfolio manager would be to buy and sell securities thus incurring commissions and lowering your return. With a fee based system your portfolio manager's and your objectives have been aligned.

There is another advantage to hiring someone to look after your investments. That person knowing that their income depends on the account performance may be tempted to look into the largest securities market in the world which is the fixed income or bond market. Yes, the debt or bond market is three times as large as the equities market. Because it is meant for investors rather than speculators, there is a liquidity problem (investors in the bond market are not there to buy and sell daily, they've made investments which they intend to hold) in that your agent may not be able to find exactly what she wants on offer, but it is so vast that she will be able to find something close to meeting your needs.

Why isn't their more retail or small investor exposure to this market? There is not enough account trading or churning to provide a good return for the "house".

The argument posed against fee only accounts by the commission driven community is that it seems irresponsible to pay someone 0.5 percent of the value of a portfolio just to maintain it. Those same trade driven stock jockeys find no harm in the mutual funds they are so willing to sell you charging 2.5 percent per year to manage your funds and more if they obtain a trailer fee. Can you go to Uber investing?

The model exists in that you can hire someone to have trading authority on your account. Note that this is not Power of Attorney as that provides the access to the assets. The account would be an online account with very low trading fees. The account would electronically notify you each time there is a transaction and you would be able to view the account on line to see what its status is and what its performance has been. At the end of the year the portfolio manager would provide you an invoice showing the year over year performance and the fee payable as a percentage of the year end value.

Technically this person, if in Ontario and some of the other provinces, would have to be registered as an advisor. This is bizarre as you are not receiving investment advice but that notwithstanding some of the regulators insist that anyone providing investment assistance and being paid for that are advisors and must be registered. This is impossible as there would be no firm that would sponsor them. The reason for this restriction is to thwart any competition for the investment industries advisors.

What I am describing is the "Uber" of the investment business. It is vehemently opposed by the existing investment structure because of the competition it will bring forth. You are placing your life in the hands of an Uber cab driver. Is that better or worse than putting your savings into the hands of an Uber portfolio manager? In fact you could split your money amongst a number of portfolio managers. Like the taxi industry the investment industry is using its regulator to oppose any encroachment on their turf but like all disruptive technologies it will win in the end.

There already is a loophole that exists. If your investment manager is not resident where you are, she can manage your account for a fee without fear of consequences from the local turf protector.

The Ten Commandments

1. Thou shalt not speculate.

2. Thou will accept a real six percent return in equity investments over the long term.

3. Thou shalt not partake of the "hot tip" or "sure thing" on any days ending in "y".

4. Thou will not buy illiquid (unsaleable) securities in the spring, summer, fall or winter of any numbered year.

5. Thou will not purchase any security that does not pay thee regularly

6. Thou will accept and believe in the "Efficient Market Thesis".

7. The investment firm and its advisor in their temple must extract as much as possible in fees from thine account.

8. The taxation authorities at their altar must extract as much as possible from the remainder of your savings.

9. There is only one angel of vengeance in the investment market and that is the Ombudsman for Banking and Investment Service, all others are false gods.

10. Thou must always fight the pestilence of inflation, management fees and trading costs, the vermin that devour savings.

You may well ask why I took over 100 pages to get to this simple solution. I wanted you to know an answer exists to, what your long term male friend was unable to tell you and why Tanya Trader went back to work on an automobile assembly line.

READING LIST

Extraordinary Popular Delusions and the Madness of Crowds by Charles Mackay

> *A classic from 1841 describing how people lost fortunes on tulip bubbles and other investing mania*

Inside the Yield Book by Homer & Leibowitz

> *A text book from the Chartered Financial Analyst's course, the book describe how bond prices are determined*

A Random Walk Down Wall Street by Burton Malkiel

> *This classic explains the efficient market thesis and why you can't beat the market*

Liars Poker by Michael Lewis

> *His best book describes the shenanigans going on behind those pillared porticos of finance*

The Creature from Jekyll Island by G.E.Griffin

> *An intriguing history of finance in the USA. How can we save J.P. Morgan's loans to Britain if the Germans win WW l? This book will explain many apparently bizarre happenings involving money including Morgan's loans.*

The Thieves of Bay Street by Bruce Livesey

> *This journalist provides a litany of abuses perpetrated on Canadian investors and the limited extent to which the institutions and perpetrators were punished.*

A History of Wealth in Canada by Gustavus Myers

> *When this American journalist fled for his safety to Canada in 1914 he was loathe to put his pen down and researched the sources of Canadian wealth from the British takeover to 1914. Canadian history isn't dull, it's not known. This book was banned in Canada until 1972.*

WHY YOU SHOULD READ THIS BOOK

The investment industry and the media have successfully managed to curtail investing in favour of trading and speculating. Your broker will never get rich if you invest but you might. The author has concluded that the most abused members of society by the investment industry are women because of their lack of financial knowledge. It is true that a major portion of the male population falls into the abuse trap but they do it knowingly.

In this book the author explains why you should invest and the barriers that will be put in place to stop you. If nothing else when you finish this book you will know the difference between a casino and a stock exchange, subtle as they may be.

About the Author,

Alex Doulis was born in Vancouver, B.C. in 1939. After graduating from the University of B.C. he worked as a geologist, mathematician and financial analyst. He obtained his Chartered Financial Analyst designation in 1978 and went on to become the top rated mining analyst in Canada.

In the 1980's he was a member of a firm that destroyed the fixed commission system and underwriting syndicates that impoverished Canadian investors and enriched the stock brokerage industry. His respect for the investor at the expense of the industry lead to him being disciplined by the Ontario Securities Commission.

He was able to retire at the age of 50 as a result of having followed the principals outlined in this book. His desire to retire was driven by the change in the investment industry from facilitating the client to enriching the firm.

His writing career began when he ran away from home at age 50 and went to sea on a sailboat in the Mediterranean. His first book, "Take Your Money & Run" on taxation was a mega best seller and was followed by a series books on financial matters and markets.

He currently lives in Toronto, where he continues to be a stone in the well-polished wing tipped shoes of the investment industry.

Also By Alex Doulis

Take Your Money & Run

My Blue Haven

The Bond's Revenge

Tackling the Taxman

Lost on Bay Street

DeCommissioned

Made in the USA
Middletown, DE
03 May 2018